Digital Dave's Computer Tips and Secrets

by Roy Davis

Edited by Tina Rathbone and Gretchen Lingham
Cover illustration by Randy Verougstraete
Inside illustrations by Sergio Ramirez
Art Direction by Leah Steward-Shahan

Every effort has been made to supply the most current
information regarding the software publishers and products
discussed in this book. However, CPE assumes no
responsibility for any infringements of patents or other
rights of third parties which would result.

ACKNOWLEDGEMENTS

I 'd like to acknowledge the following people for their invaluable help with this book:

All my loyal readers, who've supplied the ideas and inspiration for the interchange of ideas over the years.

Jack Dunning, for broadening my horizons.

My wife, who lived without me while I slaved over my column every Sunday night.

This book is
dedicated to my mom,
who got me started with
her "Hen Scratchings."

CONTENTS

INTRODUCTION

O ver the years, I've written a computer Q&A column called "Digital Dave" for San Diego's *ComputorEdge* Magazine. During that time, I've received thousands of letters from people who have been trying to get started in computers, get the best out of the computer they already have, or who need just a little bit of help. I've received a few questions where the people needed a *lot* of help, but let's save that for the last chapter, titled "Be Glad Someone Else Asked."

Many readers have told me that they save every magazine issue with my column—in case they run across the same sort of problem someday. Since I don't own any stock in a company that sells shelves, I thought maybe I should compile the best of the letters into a book, and eliminate those shelves full of back issues.

For many, a computer is very serious business, almost a religion. To others, a computer is a plaything, only slightly more intelligent than a television. I use computers at my daytime job building military communications systems—where one tiny mistake could blow up the world—but I like to play with them at home, just for the fun of it. My readers range from serious to fun-loving, and I hope my answers fit the spirit of the questions.

This book is for beginners, which means the letters were selected to answer as many first-time users' questions as space would allow.

Many books on the market, like Dan Gookin's *How to Understand and Buy Computers* and Wally Wang's *How to Understand and Find Software*, from this same publisher, take you step by step through the process of acquiring and using a computer. They give you a generous dose of facts. There are facts in this book too, but they are mixed in with opinions—both my readers' and my own. I hope these opinions give the facts another dimension and make it easier for you to get a handle on this thing called a computer.

PART I

CHAPTER 1

Laying the Groundwork

If you're new to the world of computers, you're faced with a bewildering array of choices, decisions and problems. But before we go charging off choosing between VGA and EGA displays and arguing about which CPU is best, we first have to figure out what all these confusing computer terms and acronyms mean. This is the toughest part of getting up-and-running with computers. If you can get through the alphabet soup of computer terminology, the technical stuff will be easy. I promise.

Here is a letter from a beginner stepping on the first square of the yellow brick road to computerdom. As this question and answer illustrate, as long as you break things down into smaller pieces, then try to figure out how the pieces work, you'll find computers a lot easier.

> *Dear Digital Dave,*
> *I am just beginning to learn about computers. There seem to be so many pieces that make up the puzzle. I just don't know where to start. What basically makes up a computer?*
>
> *Sandra Quintas*

Dear Sandra,

The basic parts of a computer are pretty simple. There is a Central Processing Unit (CPU) that performs all the calculations and instructions, a memory that holds data, and an Input/Output (I/O) device that enters data into the computer and reads out the results.

The other component that makes your computer work is software, which is just a list of instructions someone wrote, or programmed, to get the computer to perform some task for the user.

The CPU in a personal computer is usually one integrated circuit (newspapers call them chips) called a microprocessor. The brand of microprocessor determines which particular set of instructions it can perform, which determines what type of software will run on that computer.

The memory holds the instructions that make up the software, and the data that the software manipulates. The memory can be RAM, ROM or Magnetic. RAM, which is Random Access Memory, is a bunch of integrated circuits that only hold data when the power is on. ROM (Read Only Memory) is also an integrated circuit, but one that holds data even when the power is off.

Digital Dave's Tip

Here's a tip for those of you trying to help out newcomers to computers: When trying to teach someone a new program, have them write down all the steps to get the program started, because you know they will ask the same questions again next time. Most instruction manuals for software start out with something like, "Place your boot disk in drive A and turn on the computer." People who use computers all the time forget how important all the little things are, and how non-obvious they are to the first-time user. A good list of every step involved in booting up an application program will help make natural habits out of what is now a struggle.

Magnetic memory is usually in the form of a disk coated with the same stuff that is used on audio tape. The data is recorded and played back in rings as the disk spins past a read/write head. Not only does magnetic memory retain the data when the power is shut off, but some types of disks can be removed from the computer, with the data stored away for later use. The Input/Output devices hooked up to a home computer are generally the keyboard, video display monitor and printer. It's pretty obvious what these do. Other I/O devices can be a mouse, light pen, joystick or voice synthesizer.

So you see, when you break the computer down into these components, it makes it a lot easier to think about what each piece does. Divide and conquer.

Digital Dave

Whew! That was a bunch of things to learn in a short space. We'll talk more about all these terms throughout this book. If you need some more description, and maybe some pictures, check out the books by Dan Gookin and Wally Wang that I mentioned in the introduction.

Getting Down to Terms

Language is a process, they say. Many terms coined over the years had a perfectly logical meaning when they were freshly minted, but now are a bit quaint, if not downright misleading.

Dear Digital Dave,

I know that CPU stands for Central Processing Unit, but I hear the system box referred to as the CPU sometimes and other times a single integrated circuit chip is the CPU. Which is right?

Jamie Wyton

Dear Jamie,

The term CPU was coined back in the old days of main-frame computers, when the Central Processing Unit was a big cabinet in the middle of the computer room, and the other parts of the computer were in their own huge cabinets. The CPU did the computations that gave the computer its name. The data was stored in the main memory, which was some-times several cabinets, and there were tape drives for mass storage, which most people visualized as being the computer.

In modern computers, the CPU is usually in the same cabinet, if not on the circuit board, with the main memory and all kinds of interface hardware that used to be scattered around the computer room. That's why the term CPU could be used to describe the system box that contains most of the computer, or perhaps slightly more properly, the microprocessor chip that performs most of the tasks of a CPU.

Digital Dave

Here's another example of old computer terms coming back to haunt us. No wonder newcomers to computers think the old timers are trying to confuse them.

Dear Digital Dave,

I have heard the term "core "used to refer to the RAM in a computer. Core means the center part. If the RAM memory is the core, then how can the CPU be central?

Jorges Jasper

Dear Jorges,

The core *does* mean the center part, but not the center of the computer. Does that make any sense? Not yet.

Back when only the government and big businesses could afford computers, the main Random Access Memory (*RAM*, not *RAM memory*, one memory is enough) was made up of wires wrapped around little doughnuts of magnetic material called cores, which were the physical center of each bit of memory. Each computer would have thousands of cores.

The CPU, or Central Processing Unit, is what everything else that makes up a computer hooks up to, and usually is in the center of the computer room, and the center of attention.

Digital Dave

Dear Digital Dave,
I am trying to become computer literate and acclimate myself to the terminology (computerese) so as to intelligently converse with salespeople.
Please help my educational process by defining the following: XT, AT, clone, BIOS, modem, MS-DOS, K RAM, byte and bit, BASIC, SORT. And any other important terms I should know about. Thanks in advance for your help.
Alan Tuthill, D.C.

Dear Alan,

An *XT* is just an IBM PC with a hard disk, though there was an early PC with only five expansion slots. All recent PCs and XTs have eight slots. An *AT* is a PC compatible that uses a super-duper 80286 microprocessor. It has a slightly bigger box and runs three to 10 times faster than a PC. A *clone* is a non-IBM-manufactured PC, XT or AT, which is usually cheaper, and usually faster.

The *BIOS* is the Basic Input/Output Subsystem, which is down in the guts of the computer, and as long as it's IBM compatible, who cares? A *modem* is either an external little box or a card that plugs into one of the expansion slots inside your computer, allowing it to send and receive data over the phone lines.

MS-DOS is the white-label name for PC-DOS. Since the Disk Operating System is necessary for the operation of a computer, and the DOS has to fit the computer, it usually comes with the computer.

K RAM is a thousand, give or take a few, bytes of Random Access Memory. In computer talk a "K" means Kilo, which is a thousand everywhere else, but here it means 1,024, because computers like to count in multiples of two, and 1,024 is two times two ten times. An "M" stands for Mega, which is a million, give or take.

Byte and *bit* are pieces of data. Let's start with bit. It's a BInary digiT, which means the computer can count it as either a zero or a one. Since you can't have very many combinations of things with only zero and one, computers tend to keep groups of eight bits stuck together, which is called a byte and gives you 256 combinations of ones and zeros to play with.

BASIC is a programming language that many people really like to use. It's easy and fun, though there are reasons why it's not so great for large projects.

SORT is a generic term for putting a group of something in an order that is easier to use. For instance, a list of names in a mailing list could be sorted in alphabetical order to make it easier to spot duplicates, or you could sort by zip codes to make it easier to deliver.

I hope this has helped you get your bearings in the world of personal computers.

Digital Dave

Okay, let's leave the old computer words behind and talk about some of the newer acronyms that confuse the heck out of us. The first stop on this tour is the display monitor. For most brands of computers there are only a few unique monitor types that will work with them. For the IBM PC family there have been many standard monitors developed, and they all go by an acronym that ends in "A."

The "A" in most cases stands for *adapter*, which is the circuit card that fits inside the system cabinet of the computer. This adapter takes the instructions and data from the CPU and translates it into signals that can drive the display monitor.

Dear Digital Dave,
    Would you clarify the CGA, MCGA, MGA, EGA, PGA,
VGA alphabet soup?

Jack Jones

Dear Jack,
    It sure is tough to keep track of all the different graphics adapter cards that are available for the IBM PC family—there's a whole bowl full! Let's tackle them in chronological order.
    The MDA and the CGA were the first display cards available for the PC. The Monochrome Display Adapter (MDA) could only do characters, some of which could be used to do very limited graphics like straight lines and boxes. The Color Graphics Adapter (CGA) could do low-resolution graphics in color, or medium-resolution graphics in monochrome. I wouldn't recommend buying a computer with either of these cards in it. It's too cheap to step up to something more powerful.
    The MGA, or Monochrome Graphics Adapter, of which the Hercules version is the grandfather, is the base display adapter for most cheap PC clones these days. It does medium-resolution bit-mapped graphics in green and black, or amber and black. Since color printers haven't really made it yet, for price and quality, the MGA is the cheapest way to let you run paint and CAD (Computer Aided Design) programs with reasonable resolution.
    The Enhanced Graphics Adapter (EGA) has higher resolution and more colors available than the CGA. The new clone VGAs are about the same price as the EGA, so the EGA is also going by the wayside.
    The PGA, Professional Graphics Adapter, is strictly for those with the bucks. It has high resolution, with many colors, and requires a monitor that costs more than the car I drive.
    The VGA is IBM's new line of display adapters that comes

with the PS/2 computers. It's a little bit better than the EGA in its standard form, but most clone VGA adapters that fit PCs and ATs have SuperVGA, which is a lot better. Most software supports both EGA and VGA for color graphics.

Digital Dave

That was another tough one. If you didn't remember all those A-through-ZGAs, put a yellow sticky note on this page so when you read the chapter on video displays you can refer back to it.

Support

Here's a slightly different angle on the problems of getting started with computers: In this case, the beginner already has a computer and now has to figure out how to use it. At least he solved the problem of what computer to buy!

Dear Digital Dave,

I am the proud owner of a Macintosh SE with dual disk drives and an ImageWriter II printer. As I know very little about PCs, I'm interested in getting operational as quickly as possible.

Can you recommend a course of action? Should I attend a user group? If so, which one? Classes, where? Consultant, who? Please advise.

Sam Cafogno

Dear Sam,

How to get started? It depends on what you intend to do with your Macintosh SE with dual disk drive and Image-Writer II.

In all cases, I would get linked up with a user group or two. The support, variety of opinions and access to other resources is invaluable.

Classes? If you are going to be doing desktop publishing, attend a desktop publishing class. Computer Aided Design? A CAD class is in order. Database, word processing or spreadsheet use? Take a class on your particular application. Try to get a class that uses the Mac, but a class using other machines would still be valuable because applications tend to be similar across many types of popular computers. Check out the ads in your computer magazine or wherever computer stores advertise, as well as the offerings by the local community colleges.

A class to teach you how to use a Macintosh would not be very useful. What it takes to run a Mac you can figure out for yourself, or at least that's what Apple's advertising would have you believe. At the worst, an hour or two playing with it should get you familiar enough to run an application. If you do not have a specific application in mind, a class in a computer language like BASIC, PASCAL or C would give you a better understanding of general computer topics.

Consultants? These are the big guns saved for a special purpose or very large problems. If you are trying to computerize the inventory of a large store or are inventing a strange new business application, a hired gun is what you need to pull it together. Consultants run ads in the classified pages of computer shopper magazines and in newspapers. Also, ask around at the user group meetings for others who have hired a consultant.

Digital Dave

Training Your Computer

The more you use your computer, the more customization you want. It's extremely handy to have your computer perform certain startup functions automatically, and this can be accomplished by playing with your DOS AUTOEXEC.BAT file.

Dear Digital Dave,
   *I just bought a PC clone, so I am new to computers. I
know there is some way to log onto your computer automatically when you start it up. How do I do it?*

                                                        Ron Wolfe

Dear Ron,
   PC-DOS has a neat feature where it looks for a file called
AUTOEXEC.BAT when you boot up. You use an editor to
create or change the file, which contains commands just like
the ones you would type in from the keyboard.
   For instance, if you want to install your mouse driver so
you can use your mouse, put a line in the file like "mouse,"
which will automatically run that program. Consult your
mouse documentation for the correct command.
   If you want to set your prompt so that it shows the drive
and the subdirectory, put in a line "PROMPT PG" in the
AUTOEXEC.BAT file, too. You can do all sorts of things
with this file to save yourself some typing. Consult your DOS
manual, or a good DOS reference book like Dan Gookin's
Beginner's Guide to DOS.

                                                     Digital Dave

Well, there you have it: the short version of the basics of computers.
The terms discussed here, along with many others, will be further
explored in later chapters.

CHAPTER 2

Choosing Your Computer

This chapter is about choosing your computer. In the past, the selection process was difficult because computers from different manufacturers had very different personalities, and many incompatibilities. As computer hardware has become more powerful and cheap, there has been a blurring of the lines between different brands. For instance, the graphics-based drawing programs that were closely associated with the Macintosh have come to the IBM PC in a big way.

The powerful spreadsheet and database programs used in businesses and run on PCs can now run on Macs. In fact, programs like Microsoft *Word* and *Excel*, a word processor and spreadsheet, function almost identically on the Mac and PC, and can swap data back and forth. All of this has made the selection process easier and brought more everyday people into the world of computers.

That's not to say that you should just run out and buy the first computer a salesperson shows you. A little bit of work on your part will pay off in a computer that better fits your needs and your pocketbook.

Decisions, Decisions

Now it's time to start zeroing in on that computer of your dreams. The first thing to figure out is just what you intend to do with it. Do you want a super small laptop computer to stuff in your briefcase for those business trips, a power CPU with a high-resolution monitor for Computer Aided Design work, or do you just want a machine on which you can play games?

Dear Digital Dave,
    I am about to purchase my first computer and I'm not sure what I want to buy. I've heard that IBMs are the way to go, but I like playing games and I'm not sure if the IBM can cut it. Any advice you could give would sure be appreciated. Thanks.

                                                          Mark Larry

Dear Mark,
    Boot up one of the big-name flight simulators on an AT with a VGA screen, then tell me the IBM clones can't hack it. It's true the original 4.77 MHz PC was a dog, but the clone makers have made the 12 MHz AT the entry-level machine these days.
    Go down to your local software store, one with computers so customers can try out their wares, and spend some time getting a feel of what's available for the various types of machines. Try a couple different stores, since some cater to one machine. When you find the kind of software selection and performance you want, buy the machine supporting that software.

                                                          Digital Dave

Dear Digital Dave,
    Should I buy a IBM PC or an AT clone?
                                                          Herman Cadrick

Dear Herman,
    It's getting hard to justify buying a PC these days, the ATs are so inexpensive. The '486 is on the horizon and the '386

is getting cheaper in the guise of the '386SX, so the '286 is becoming the entry-level processor. The '286 is the AT processor. The poor old '8088 used in the PC and XT is on fire sale.

If you're going to limit your computer to a cheap PC clone with a 20MB hard disk, a monographics adapter and one or two floppy drives, and you're only going to do simple word processing or business tasks, you might be happy with a PC. If you're going to do fancy graphics, especially in color, invest in the fastest AT chassis you can afford. Put off some of the add-on goodies until later, if necessary.

If you're going to be playing with large databases, make sure the AT you buy has a big and fast hard disk. Those 65 millisecond pigs belong on PCs, not ATs. Twenty-eight milliseconds is more like it.

If you compare the price of the bare-bones chassis, the PC or XT looks much cheaper than the AT. Add in the hard drive, color display and adapter card, 2400 Baud modem, printer and a desk to put it on, and you find the difference is not so great.

Digital Dave

Buying a Computer for Your Child

Some people want to buy a computer for their little ones to help out with their school work. These parents will see the low-priced "home computer" in Toys-R-Us, and think that the $395 price tag will just about cover it. Guess again. What about a color display monitor and a disk drive or two? And the kids can't turn in homework done on the computer unless there's a printer.

When you stack it all up, for the same price as a "toy" you can have a real personal computer with a lot more software available and much more growth capacity. For those on a tight budget, there's always the used computer market. But again, watch out for the extras it takes to make a whole system. Beware of pouring a bucket of money into a dead-end system.

> *Dear Digital Dave,*
>   *I'm a single mom, and I'd like my two children, ages 6 and 12, to have the advantage of a computer in the home to keep up with school work.*
>   *I know nothing about computers. What should I do? Also, I don't have much money to spend.*
>   *Mariann Parker*

Dear Mariann,

The 6-year-old is in the prime Apple II age. There are a ton of educational programs for that age group and computer type. The 12-year-old is getting out of the "John has 3 apples, Mary has 2 apples, how many apples do John and Mary have?" level of most educational packages.

Used Apples with monitors and disk drives (both necessary for the computer to be useful) are hovering around the $1,000 mark. Then you need a printer. No bargains there.

The Apple IIgs is a neat machine for the kids, but it's way over-priced and a dead-end system. Any significant upgrades when the kids reach high school would require starting over with new hardware and throwing away all your software.

The Apple Macintosh is cute, and powerful enough for even college work, but again it's probably out of your price range.

A brand-new PC clone can be had for half the price of a used Apple II, but it will have no color. To interest kids, the clone would need at least a color monitor and video card, which brings the price up to about $750.

Yes, there is educational software for the PC, but not as much as for the Apple. What there is tends to be of much higher quality than Apple software. PC educational software takes advantage of the more powerful processor and higher

takes advantage of the more powerful processor and higher resolution color display, too. Also, the PC has more growth capacity—such as for word processors to write term papers in high school.
Your best bet is to talk with as many parents who work with their computers and kids as possible. One place to find them would be the Beginners Users Group of your local computer club, where you can learn from the ground up. Check your local computer magazine for meeting times and places.

Digital Dave

Teaching an Old Computer New Tricks

Is it worth it to pick up an older computer model at a "bargain" price? I get many letters from first-time computer buyers who have their eyes on a computer model that's been around quite some time. These older machines fill the used computer classified ads in almost every newspaper and shopper magazine.
The trouble is, first-time buyers don't understand what it takes to make a *complete* system, so they make an initial investment, then are forced to spend a lot more than they intended. And having spent all that money, they still end up with a dead-end machine that can't be upgraded to run the latest software.

Dear Digital Dave,
I was just given an Apple II Plus, two disk drives, an FX70 Printer and DOS 3.3. The computer has a RAM16 board in slot one (64K, I believe, but I'm not sure). I have no documentation or software. Moreover, I've had no luck in finding any for a unit this old.
Can the II Plus be expanded to run current IIc/IIe software, plus PRODOS? Can the keyboard be expanded to, say, 5060 configuration?

As this is my first computer, would I be wiser to sell it and put my money into an IBM-compatible unit? I'll use it for business applications only.

                                                        John Willis, Jr.

Dear John,
    The first thing you must do is narrow down the purpose of your computer usage. A wide range of business applications exist. For example, the factory where my brother works uses those $39 Sinclair computers as controllers for their automated equipment!
    Now, if you're going to do some simple spreadsheets ,or a very small index-card type database, then you'll get by with an Apple II Plus with two floppy disk drives. If you want to do even a medium-small database, or want to have a first-class word processor with a built-in dictionary, then you'll want a machine with more RAM and a hard disk. The Apple II Plus does not lend itself to expansion much beyond what you have.
    Since you already have the hardware, I would go to a few user's group meetings and try to find others who run similar applications. Pick their brains for all they are worth. That's why people go to such meetings.
    At the meetings, get your hands on the public domain software (free or very cheap) that applies to your business. Work with these programs to learn more about computers.
    The investment of your time will give you a better understanding of computers, and will have value no matter what computer you end up with. On the other hand, don't make any large investments of money in hardware or software until you have a pretty good understanding of your computer's limits.
    Check the computer classified ads for the going rate on used Apples. You might be able to sell your gift and use the money toward a system more suitable for business use, like an IBM PC clone or a Macintosh.

                                                        Digital Dave

I get the same kinds of questions all the time, and I get accused of Apple bashing, but people keep getting trapped with a big investment in a very old computer design and then ask me for advice on how to get their Apple to do the things that they see the newer, more powerful machines doing. Can the venerable, old computers still around do things the new machines were designed for? Usually, but not nearly so well, or as fast.

Dear Digital Dave,
   I have an Apple IIe and would like to find a good desktop publishing program. My printer is a Panasonic KXP1091. Has anyone found something to meet this need?
   From what I read, the best desktop publishing programs are for the Apple Macintosh or the IBM PC—and a good printer, such as a laser printer, that costs about $4,000. I can't afford this.
   Has anyone tried the NEC P6 Pinwriter with a desktop publishing program? A consumer's guide recommended it. I will look for your suggestions. Thanks.

Rosemarie Dion

Dear Rosemarie,
   New desktop publishing programs are popping up every week, and the combinations of hardware they support are so varied it's hard to make recommendations. You're right about the good stuff showing up on the Mac and the PC. It's only a matter of time before every computer model will have a passable desktop publishing package available.
   You are also right about the printer being an important part of the selection. The fanciest program is only as good as the printed output, and the laser printers with their 300 dot-per-inch resolution look very good.
   There is a way out for those on a tight budget. Many stores that provide copying services are installing laser printers and

computers which you can rent to make your final version. First you use your dot matrix printer to do your proof copies and get everything just right. Then you hightail it down to the local copy joint and run out the final printout on their laser printer.

The problem with using the copy joint's laser printer is that they probably only have a Macintosh hooked up to it. It looks like you're in for the purchase of a Mac, if you're going to get serious about desktop publishing.

I have an NEC P6 printer plugged into my PC clone. I've tried it with the *PFS: First Publisher* program, and it works very well. It emulates the Epson FX series of printers, so the resolution is great, for a dot matrix printer.

Digital Dave

Types of Ports

When you're making your computer-buying decision, you'll eventually have to consider all the plug-in cards that provide interfaces to other devices. These interfaces are called *ports*, and you have to know which one is which to decide what you want installed immediately, and which ones can wait until later.

Dear Digital Dave,
What's the difference between a serial port, a parallel port and a game port?

Jackie Fee

Dear Jackie,
Basically, a serial port is for a modem, a parallel port for printers, and a game port for joysticks. The confusion comes in when you have a printer that hooks up to a serial port.

First, we have to remember that computers work with bunches of bits, called *bytes*. A bit is a BInary digiT (a one or a zero), and when you put eight of them together, you have 256 possible combinations of ones and zeros.

The characters are assigned to certain combinations of ones and zeros, called ASCII codes. This is how the various letters, numbers and graphics characters are handled by your computer. Serial ports deal with characters one bit at a time. This is ideal for modems, because they can only send one bit at a time across the telephone line. Back in the old days it was common to hook a printer directly up to a modem for remote printing. That's why some printers have a modem-type serial interface. This practice is falling by the wayside.

Most printers are right next to the computer that is driving them, so it's no big deal to run eight wires (all bundled up in a cable), one for each bit in a byte. This makes a simpler, faster interface for printers. It's called a parallel interface because the bits all travel simultaneously, in parallel.

Another big difference between the serial and parallel ports is that the serial port is designed to handle data traffic in both directions, while the parallel port is unidirectional: from the computer to the printer.

The game port is a completely different beast. It measures the electrical resistance of some device, like a joystick or a game paddle. The paddle is the easiest to understand. It has a knob similar to a volume control. When you rotate the knob, you vary the resistance, which the game port measures. Your game program then reacts by moving something on the screen.

A joystick is nothing more than two paddles mounted in one box, which has a mechanical gadget that turns one volume control when you move the stick back and forth, and the other volume control when you move it up and down.

Digital Dave

Compatibility

Back in the bad old days of IBM PC clones, a lot of junk on the market wouldn't run the same programs as the true-blue IBM PC.

Since then, a few companies have figured out how to make the internal software (called the BIOS ROM) truly compatible without infringing on any copyrights. Fortunately, these few companies have sold their ROMs to everyone else who builds decent computers.

Dear Digital Dave,
    I've heard that problems of compatibility, specifically on IBM compatibles, are partly due to the use of a ROM BIOS chip which is not compatible with IBM. I understand that the Phoenix brand chip is considered to be the "most" compatible. Is this correct?
    I have not had any compatibility problems with my no-name, but I also don't run a lot of different software.
                                                    Harry Bishop

Dear Harry,
    Most of the recent clone BIOS chips that come in machines from reputable computer stores have been about as compatible as you can be. I won't say that about some of the junk that Looney Larry's Stereo Shop sells. Make sure you buy from a seller that knows what he is selling and backs the sale up with service and warranty.
                                                    Digital Dave

Dear Digital Dave,
    The American Research Corporation (ARC) BIOS is very good. In fact, they have contracted with Microsoft to produce ARC DOS, which is MS-DOS with the ARC name and logo on it.
    The machines are also very good. Mine was dropped off the back of a delivery truck. After putting the hard disk back to its original position (it was at a 45-degree angle) and re-inserting the floppies and all the other boards, it booted right

up. I reformatted the hard disk with no problems at all. The case is kind of warped but works just fine.

Jeff Collins

Dear Jeff,

Thanks for the report. I also have the ARC BIOS in my clone, though it's an old version, and haven't had compatibility problems.

By the way, I would have refused delivery of a computer that had been dropped in shipment. It might work now, but the hard drive might have been damaged on some inside sectors that you won't see until you fill it up. The carrier has insurance to cover such things.

Digital Dave

SR

I never thought IBM would come out with a line of computers incompatible with their own line of PCs and ATs, but surprisingly they have: the Personal System 2, or PS/2.

Dear Digital Dave,
    I just got my IBM clone last month. I can't tell you how long I wanted one. Soon after getting it, I began hearing about the new System 2 and how it would be the new standard.
    I used to have a TI 99/4A and sorely watched that model become obsolete—selling for pennies compared to what it cost me. Is history repeating itself again?
    It would seem to me that so many companies are involved with ventures relating to the IBM clone that it would go on forever. But I thought the same about the Atari 2600 video game system. Will my new system soon become "old"?
                                                    Dennis Hunt

Dear Dennis,
    Your PC clone design is old. Having been brought to market in 1981, it has existed for more than half the history of microprocessors, on which the personal computers are based. The conservative design and the open architecture of both the software and the hardware made it the standard it is.
    My Chevy Van is over 10 years old, but vans haven't really changed much. It still hauls my camping equipment to the mountains. Fancy four-wheel drive rigs I see around now make me drool—but the old van still gets me there.
    The new IBM PCs are big news, but the new operating system that takes advantage of the new hardware is not even available yet. I would say it will be a year before you and I are even able to use one, and another year before a decent base of software has developed.
    The major advantage to the new Personal Systems will be the connectivity to IBM mainframes. I don't happen to have

a mainframe laying around my house, so I'm not too excited about upgrading my computer.

I think IBM will take a lot of corporate sales away from the clone makers, but you and I will be buying the off-brand clones for quite some time, and getting good software support because there are so many of us.

Digital Dave

Some Final Words of Advice

I've preached and preached about researching your prospective computer purchase before you make your selection, but there are those who insist on going off half-cocked. They buy a core of a computer, usually an older CPU for cheap, then spend 10 times that amount trying to play catch-up with the new stuff. It's cheaper to buy the basic CPU with more than you need, then add the peripherals as you can afford them.

Dear Digital Dave,
I am somewhat new to the PC world, so I've started out like many others before me. I go into computer stores and touch everything I see. I mean, how else is one to learn if he hasn't been spoken to by a salesperson?
Well, the local computer store nearest me is Store X. My dad came home from his monthly fishing trip early last week carrying an IBM PC. He retired in March from the carpenter's union (you really need to know all this background). If there ever was a computer illiterate, it's Pops.
Anyway, he surprised me with this true-blue IBM PC. He said, "Hey, what'ya say you and me fix this thing up?" Now, you have to understand something up front: this PC only has a motherboard and a case. I started in on the "it has no cards of any kind, nor does it have memory" typical, discouraging kinda statements.
That didn't work. He reminded me of a project he and I

*tackled a few years before, when I had to have a BMW 2002.
I knew it wasn't going to be easy to put it together the way
I wanted it, but my dad gave me a lot of help. OK, so it wasn't
a 528e, but it was still a BMW and it was what I wanted.*

*Anyway, my dad said, "Well, we could work on [the
computer] together, and maybe we'll both learn something."*

*So, even if it has a speed of 4.77 MHz, it's still a true-blue
IBM, and with all the add-on boards and big hard drives
we'll want, it looks like a project that my dad and I can sink
out teeth into—not to mention a great deal of money.*

*I would like to add an Intel 30386 board, an 80MB hard
drive, a 5¼-inch, 1.2MB floppy drive, and a 3½-inch,
1.44MB floppy drive—as well as an AST SixPack Plus card,
and maybe a Paradise Plus VGA monitor card.*

*Please advise me on a few things. First, will my hard-
drive controller handle my two floppies? And does the fact
that this IBM PC has an 8-bit bus make a difference? I have
already purchased a 200 Watt Turbo Cool power supply.*

*I realize I am asking a lot of questions that maybe my
local computer store could answer, but those boneheads
over at Store X tell me to trash what little I have and start
with a motherboard that already has a 20 MHz '386 on it.*

*What they don't understand is that I want this to be a
project for my dad and me, and I don't want to lay out $800
to $1,200 all at once. So, please, any information you care
to share with me would be greatly appreciated.*

C. Donald Davis, Jr.

Dear Donald,

Those guys at Store X are really trying to steer you
straight. Two hulks of 8-bit PCs, one of which is a five-slot,
true-blue IBM, sit in the junk pile in my garage. There is no
future in trying to upgrade them to the level you describe.

How about adjusting the scope of the project to be more

appropriate for a beginner on a small budget? First, get the thing going on its own power. The 8088 processor is no speed demon, but it runs, so leave it alone for now.

Those '386 plug-in cards are more expensive than a bare-bones '386 clone motherboard. Besides, they require a funky kludge to the operating system to work, which doesn't work with some software. When the old man's a computer whiz, and needs the speed, build a new machine around a real '386 motherboard.

Big hard drives, like 80MB, are usually fast, and very expensive. How about a Seagate ST-225, which came in true-blue machines (among others)? It's good for 20MB, and a lot cheaper. The standard setup for PCs (actually the name of the machine with a hard drive is *XT*) was a dual floppy controller and a separate hard-drive controller.

One 360K floppy was the standard setup. PC-class software comes on 5¼-inch 360K floppies, so a 1.2MB drive is a waste on a PC.

You seem to be in love with the name-brand nameplate on your toys. I guess I'm the opposite extreme. Two of my three desktop PCs don't even have nameplates!

Finding parts on the used market would be an exciting and inexpensive way to go. Check out the classified ads in your local computer magazine, or even advertise for what you want to buy.

Computer swapfests are also a fun way to find the odds and ends to build your computer. Look for upcoming events.

The one area where you could invest in the latest hardware would be the display adapter and monitor. VGA cards that work in both 8-bit and 16-bit chassis are getting to be the norm. You won't lose a thing when you upgrade to a real '386.

When you have the basic machine to the point where it's actually working, and you want to move up, donate it to a charitable group, write it off on your taxes, and use the knowledge you gained to build a top-of-the-line machine.

I hate to sound like a snob about this, but putting a '386
in a PC chassis is like trying to put a Diesel engine out of a
bus into your 2002. Sure you could make it work, but why?
It isn't going to be practical, or very fun to drive.

Digital Dave

If you really want to improve your computer's performance, it's time
to retire that undersized CPU and step up to a machine appropriate
for all the plug-in goodies.

Dear Digital Dave,
My computer is an IBM PCjr. It has the Quadram
expansion chassis, the second disk drive and a 384K
memory board. I have the IBM 128K sideboard, too, which,
with the 128K internal memory the jr already has, gives me
640K.
My question is, can I go beyond 640K? I've heard from
the PCjr national users group that it's possible by using the
extra memory as a RAM drive-only memory. But they're
unable to tell me how, or where to get the extra memory
from.
Any information you can give me will be passed on to
the rest of the local PCjr users group. Don't bother asking
IBM. It took them years before they would admit the jr went
up to 640K. They still claim a 2400 baud modem won't work
on the jr. We know differently!

Rick Arnold

Dear Rick,
I'm sure you could get an EMS (Extended Memory Standard) board, like an AboveBoard or RAMpage, to work with
your PCjr, though the technical details are beyond the scope
of this book. Let's concentrate on the question: Why bother?
If you have disk drives that only hold 360K, then the
largest program that can be loaded takes up only about half

your available memory. Why not use a RAM disk program that uses the upper part of the memory you already have? There are RAM disk programs available in the public domain, so the price is right.

I recently put a 1 Megabyte EMS memory board in my PC clone, and, quite frankly, it really hasn't sped things up much. You need a hard disk to have enough data on-line to need a RAM disk outside the 640K DOS limit, and the hard disk is much faster than the floppies, so you don't need the RAM disk speed so much.

What this all comes down to, is that an investment in a hard disk would give you more speed, plus much more storage to boot.

Digital Dave

Here's the other side of the coin. The fancy box doesn't make the computer run faster.

Dear Digital Dave,
    Are the new tower-type PCs more powerful than the standard lay-down desk units? How?

Tony Ferraci

Dear Tony,

    The tower cases hold exactly the same hardware as the desktop units, except maybe a little more of it, so the performance is the same. The tower units usually have a bigger power supply and a few more spots to install disk drives.

    This is useful for situations like local area network (LAN) file servers or engineering workstations that need lots of disk space, but it's more of a status symbol than anything else for the rest of us.

    On the other hand, my AT is sitting on its side on the floor by my desk, so it looks like a tower!

Digital Dave

We've looked at some of the different aspects of computer selection.
Let's pull it together.

Dear Digital Dave,
   There are lots of IBM compatibles or look-alikes around.
How can I judge which are of reasonable quality and
compatibility? In other words, I am looking for the least
expensive route that will give me IBM functionality. I ap-
preciate your help.

Amrum Lakritz

Dear Amrum,
   First of all, we have to figure out what we mean by "IBM
functionality." Big Blue makes several different PC models
with different features, including four different display adapters. IBM isn't even compatible with itself!
   True functionality is found in the software. Find one or
more programs that do what you want to do with a computer,
then pick a piece of hardware that supports that software.
   If you are into arcade games, a color graphics adapter and
a compatible BIOS is what you want. It's real easy to find
out; just play the games on the machine in the showroom.
   Most computer stores won't mind you taking it for a test
drive. (Watch out for the salesman who tries to put a few
bucks on the game. Those guys are pretty good. What do you
think they do in the slack time between customers?)
   I digress. The biggest difficulty is in the area of programs
written in BASIC. The IBM PC uses a BASIC that is partly
in the ROM chips in the computer. Most BASIC programs
that have been compiled try to use the pieces of BASIC that
are supposed to be in ROM on a genuine, true-blue IBM. They
don't find any if it is running on a clone.
   My experience has been that the PC clones sold by
reputable dealers are pretty compatible, while most of the

el-cheapo clones sold by people who don't sell computers for a living are a real problem.

Ask around for experience with a model you intend to buy. Go to a users group meeting, and listen to the horror stories and the fairy tales. You'll have to sort out which is which, but you'll get more information than you can use.

The only other trick I can suggest is to ask the computer seller for an itemized list of all of the major components, with model number and manufacturer. If the seller can't come up with this information, he doesn't know what he's selling, and surely couldn't fix it if there were a problem.

Digital Dave

You have a computer model and configuration in mind now. Where are you going to buy it? Here are some points concerning the computer store's services.

Dear Digital Dave,
I have recently bought a "local IBM clone."
What is worrying me is the phrase "burn-in time" that I read a lot in advertisements. What does this mean (in terms a novice or intermediate user would understand), and of what consequence is a lower burn-in time?
I hope I didn't find out about this burn-in thing too late (since I have already made my purchase)!
Pam Lopes

Dear Pam,
If you have used your new computer for more than a few days, you've already passed the burn-in period. Most failures of complex electronics occur in the first few hours of operation.

Most reputable manufacturers run their products for several hours or a few days to get their products past this point, and save a lot of hassle with having to make warranty repairs.

Since most local PC clones are assembled by the local store, the store is the manufacturer. It's a trade-off between just sending products out the door and having to fix the ones that fail, or burning in the products to catch most of the failures before the customers take them home.

I purchased my CP/M machine mail-order over 5 years ago and never had a problem. I was lucky! My printer died after one week, and was promptly replaced by the local computer store. If I'd purchased that printer from a mail-order catalog, I would have had to wait at least two weeks to get the faulty printer back to the seller and get the new one delivered. It broke the day before a big report was due, and I got it back on-line in time.

The Seagate hard drive in my PC clone got flaky after two months. Again the local store came to the rescue and replaced it, no charge, no questions asked. It pays to spend a few more dollars locally—so you'll have a store handy where you can bring your problems back.

The burn-in is a help, but it's no replacement for a good warranty.

Digital Dave

Dear Digital Dave,

This letter concerns a problem perhaps more moral than technical. Care to be "Dear Abby" for a moment? Almost two years ago, I bought a '286 machine from a dealer whose primary business is selling printer ribbons and the like, but who also puts together "custom-tailored," reasonably priced computers.

The resident technoid discussed my needs and budget with me, and we came up with an acceptable combination of hardware and price. Included in the list was an 8/10/12 MHz motherboard and 640K of 100 nanosecond RAM. I recall specifically paying extra to get the recommended 100 ns chips instead of 120 ns chips. The receipt I have specifies the agreed-upon hardware.

Recently I opened the case to upgrade the memory to 1MB. I found all the RAM chips save one marked -12, which apparently means 120 ns. The one exception was marked -3. Also, the jumper-setting options on the ELT 286-B 1000-SM motherboard indicate that it can be set to run at 8 or 10 MHz, but not the 12 MHz indicated on my receipt.

When I mentioned this apparent deception to a relative that works in the OEM end of the industry, he told me, "Now you know how the computer industry works."

So, to the questions! Have the slower chips made a significant difference in the performance of my machine (used mostly for word processing)? Might the one oddball chip marked "-3-" have contributed to the occasional malfunctions I have suffered while working on very large documents in WordPerfect?

Would the dealer really have deceived me just to save a few bucks on the RAM and motherboard? Does the industry really work this way, or only shops that primarily sell printer ribbons? And, finally, in the eternal scheme of things, does this really matter?

Ernest Eidolon

Dear Ernest,

Does it matter? Of course it matters! You've been ripped off, and there is no excuse for it. Unfortunately, this is pretty much how the bottom end of the computer retailing business is run.

That's why I don't buy at the store with the best price. If they are the cheapest, they had to give up something. Now maybe they didn't rip you off intentionally. Maybe there is someone out there who is wondering why his 10 MHz AT with 120 nanosecond RAM chips (which was really supposed to be yours) runs faster than the next guy's, because it's really running at 12 MHz. But you got ripped off just the same, by dealing with people who saved money by being overworked and sloppy.

The difference in performance between a 10 MHz and 12 MHz AT is very slight, especially for text-based applications, but there is a difference. I would be more upset about the assorted RAM chips, which means either they had trouble and had to replace at least one chip, or they used whatever chips were laying around. Both scenarios scare me. Using different chips is technically okay, but indicates crummy work ethics.

If the printer-ribbon store people were not careful about putting together your computer, they probably were not very careful about selecting sources for the components of your system. There is a lot of junk out there. That's why I shop at the larger, locally owned computer stores. They're big enough that they can't afford to do a bad job, and small enough to be able to yell at the boss if there's a problem.

Digital Dave

Dear Digital Dave,

We purchased a Challenger Computer AT-286 (or so it says when it boots up). The name on the outside is Turbo/AT Beltron. I can't seem to find out this company's location so I can procure an owner's manual.

Could you ask around and see if you can come up with a lead as to where these people might be? I would be eternally grateful.

Sue Williamson

Dear Sue,

I'm sure I know where these people are (Taiwan), and what you are going to get for an owner's manual (nothing). Them's the breaks in the clone world.

On the other hand, IBM just bought a bunch of AT clones

by Acer, which they shipped to fill a government contract for IBM AT computers. IBM said they were exact clones, so the government shouldn't have a problem with that. What's good enough for IBM should be good enough for you. This means that the technical books about the PC and AT that are available in bookstores should be pretty close for your clone. I've found this to be generally true.

There are many books on the market that do a much better job of explaining your computer than typical owner's manuals. Peter Norton's *Inside the IBM PC* explains the hardware pretty well, and I have a whole shelf full of books that teach you more than you care to know about DOS.

The Challenger name in the bootup message is part of what's known as the BIOS ROM. This was either put in the machine overseas or stuck in at the store where you bought the computer.

All of that is fine, as far as I'm concerned, but there is no excuse for the lack of a decent owner's manual. I know that's the way it is, but it shouldn't be, for their sake! It saves the company money to put out a good manual so new owners won't be calling for customer support, or returning their machines when nothing is really wrong with them.

I would go back to the store that sold you the computer and harass them into giving you an owner's manual. It should at least give you the machine-specific things, such as the location and settings for the configuration switches on the main board. You might have to make due with a photocopy, but you don't intend to display it on your cocktail table in the living room, right?

And don't forget information on all the plug-in boards. A million times I have gotten stuck trying to fix a computer problem because the owner didn't have the manual for that $35 multi-I/O card.

Digital Dave

Summary

I hope this chapter has given you some pointers on selecting a computer from the vast range available out there. The different brands and models of computers have many things in common, and many differences. High price is no guarantee of a good selection. On the other hand, there is no such thing as too much computer power.

Spend some time learning about computers, and ask the people you know with similar interests. They might only be able to tell you what not to do, based on their mistakes, but it's one way to whittle down the alternatives. There is no absolutely right selection, only different shades of good and bad choices.

Just don't get caught in the cycle of waiting for the next major hardware or software breakthrough. I jumped in and spent two month's salary on a 64K CP/M machine way back when. I sold that machine for $200 recently, but it paid for itself several times over in the learning and the improved opportunities it gave me. I have spent a lot of money on computers over the years, but a lot less than on that rust bucket sitting in my driveway.

Of course, I've spent a lot more time learning how to use my computers than I ever did on learning to drive. It's just a different kind of investment.

CHAPTER 3

Software Decisions

A computer is just a pile of dumb hardware until you add the software that tells it what to do. That jumble of microprocessors, RAMs and floppy disks is useless without an application program to tell the hardware to do the task you've assigned.

As we discussed in the first chapters, as the power of personal computer hardware has increased, application software has become very similar on various hardware platforms. (A hard-ware platform is a fancy name for the various brands of computer hardware that run a specific operating system, like MS-DOS.)

Getting started with computers is a process of first deciding what to do with one, finding the software that does it, then finding the hardware to support that software. First let's visit with someone who has suffered the difficulties of choosing software. Then we will take a look at some ways to ease the pain of it all.

Dear Digital Dave,

You recommend that people first try a program, and when satisfied, buy the machine to run it. Simple? No!

To really appreciate a program, one must work with it and know what it can do. Being told is nice, but actually doing it is better. To properly evaluate a program, one must be able to compare it with other programs. This software-

familiarization process is not accomplished in five minutes. It's the same way with hardware.

To be frank, it has taken me at least a year to really function in dBASE, *to make it do what I want it to do. The other pre-packaged* dBASE *programs they gave me didn't always work, and when they did work, they didn't always do what I wanted.*

Bob Adams

Dear Bob,

Thanks for the thoughts on buying software.

As you described, selecting a piece of software is quite a commitment, and not something to do just in a computer store showroom. I suggest reading reviews, talking to knowledgeable friends and others at club meetings, and narrowing the field down to just a few. The final selection might require that you borrow or rent a computer and the software.

I spent considerable time learning *dBASE II* back in the old days. We had committed the entire parts system of our factory to *dBASE II* on a CP/M machine. When *dBASE II* came out for the PC-DOS world, I hooked one of each machine together and transferred the data and command files we had generated.

And guess what? They worked with absolutely no modification! But only because we used very simple screen displays that were common to both machines. Updating to *dBASE III* took a bit more work, but those old data files live on. I'm just glad we picked a solid software package to begin with. The application has transcended the hardware!

Digital Dave

The most important thing to remember is that the most expensive part of owning a computer is the time and effort involved in learning to use a particular application program, and the time it takes to enter data into the program.

In this example, a commitment was made to Ashton Tate's *dBASE* line of database managers. We'll talk about what a database manager does a bit later. The point is, effort was expended over several years to use this product, and because the manufacturer provided an upgrade path, the users could make that effort pay off over a long term, past generations of computer hardware and operating system releases.

So, how do we go about picking the software? A favorite method of mine has paid off time after time: reading books about programs that interest me. I know it seems silly to purchase books for programs that you will never own, but it's the quickest way I know to learn what a program can do without having a tutor sitting there with you, or a copy of the program to play with. The only problem is that I've run out of bookshelves, and the ones I do have are sagging.

Earlier, I implied that the best way to learn a program is to have a copy of it, with someone there to teach it to you. Yes, there are seminars given by the people who sell the programs, assuming you are looking at the expensive end of the software market. But those tend to be more sales pitch than genuine evaluation experience.

And what if you just want to purchase a word processor with which to write the Great American Novel? Go to a users group meeting for your brand of computer, and if you play your cards right, someone will take you under their wing and give you an in-depth trial spin in the program you're interested in. Most large metropolitan areas and even many small towns have computer clubs with

Digital Dave's Tip

Many programs come with a file named something like "READ.ME" on the disk. This file usually contains text concerning information that is too new to have been included in the printed manual. Print this file out and put it with your instruction manual, so you have all the latest information in one readable place.

Those READ.ME, or maybe README.DOC, files can be very important, so don't pass them up

special interest groups where new and experienced users can get together and help each other.

Which Program Is Which

So how do you tell if you have the latest and greatest version of a program? Read on.

Dear Digital Dave,
   This may be a dumb question, but what do the numbers mean in program names, like WordPerfect 5.1? *My Tandy has DOS version 2.11.22. What do those numbers mean?*
                                                        Georgia Forness

Dear Georgia,
   Those digits attached to the program name are known as the version number. They let you know if you have the latest and greatest copy of the program.
   An increase in the first digit means that there have been major changes to the program. For instance, if you have version 1.34 of *Program-X*, and you purchase an update to version 2.0, you'll usually receive a disk with the new program, plus a whole new manual, because they've changed the way the program works. Throw out the old one and start over.
   The digits after the period keep track of minor changes. The manual usually stays the same, with maybe a couple of pages of notes on the changes to explain the differences.
   If there is a letter after the version number, or in the case of your Tandy DOS, a third set of digits after a second period, there have been some really minor bug fixes, which usually don't make a difference to the casual user. The changes are usually noted in a READ.ME file on the program disk.
   Now you might think that having the latest and greatest version of the program would be a good idea in all cases.

However, there are a few instances I can think of where you might stick with the old trusty version for a while. When most major DOS version changes are made, such as from 2.12 to 3.0, there is reason to mistrust the newfangled one. Many people will wait until the release of version 3.1, which indicates the first re-release of the DOS with some field use under its belt.

Another reason to hold on to an old version, especially when it is public domain software, is "creeping feature-itis." I use version 1.26 of the *KERMIT* file-transfer program because it is only a 16K file, which loads and runs very quickly. Versions starting with 2.0 are 64K or larger, and take forever to load. The new one paints a much fancier screen display, but the old one works faster.

The last reason I can think of to hold on to an old version is to stay compatible with data and command files. Lotus *1-2-3* is a famous one. When they upgraded to version 2.0, they caused some incompatibilities with data and macro files generated for earlier versions. Many people have decided to stick with the old version rather than go through the hassle of upgrading.

Digital Dave

Sometimes the version numbers are not enough to identify which is which. There are programs that are sold under different brand names, but are identical.

Dear Digital Dave,
   What exactly is the difference between MS-DOS and IBM's PC-DOS?

Al Holloway

Dear Al,
   There really is no difference between MS-DOS and PC-DOS themselves, but there is a difference in the things that

come with them. MS-DOS is the generic flavor Disk Operating System, while PC-DOS is the IBM brand name for the same thing.

Microsoft, hence *MS*-DOS, sells the operating system to many computer manufacturers, including IBM. The manufacturers add their own machine-specific BIOS (Basic Input/Output Subsystem). In the case of many PC clones, the machine is so close that PC-DOS will run on it. I use PC-DOS 3.3 on mine.

PC-DOS comes with BASICA, which only works with the BASIC in the ROM chips found only in a true-blue IBM PC. There is a very cheap version of DOS that comes with a FORMAT program that is much nicer to use than the one that comes with PC-DOS. FORMAT is DOS version-specific, and I use a later version now, so I don't use that off-brand FORMAT anymore.

Digital Dave

Software Tips

When you're first starting out, you need all the help you can get, and you need it handy.

Here is a good tip from a reader who doesn't want you to wipe out the master disks of that expensive new program by doing something dumb.

Dear Digital Dave,

If the first instruction you get when unpacking a new piece of software is to make backup copies, why don't they tell you to put write-protect tabs on the diskettes, just in case you get "TARGET" and "SOURCE" disks mixed up when using any of the disk-copying utilities?

Carol Westheimer

Dear Carol,

That's a good point. Especially on a machine with low memory, where you have to swap disks a few times, it's easy to wipe out your source (original) disk. I always put the write-protect tabs on first. Well, almost always. Some companies, like Microsoft, have their act together. They use disks that don't even have a notch in the disk to put a tab over. There is no way to write to a disk like this and destroy it without changing the circuitry inside the disk drive.

I wish more companies would show such class and distribute their software on notchless diskettes.

Digital Dave

Here's a concept that's been used by programmers for years, but only recently has been introduced into the user interface of software applications.

Dear Digital Dave,

I've seen the term "macro" used with several programs. I've used many of these programs, but still I don't understand what a macro is. Can you explain it in terms I can understand?

Robert Browning

Dear Robert,

The concept is very simple. You are probably expecting it to be complicated, but it isn't. Macros are simple but powerful tools.

A macro is a preset pattern or template that can change in detail when it is used. The use of a macro saves having to copy a series of commands over and over.

Suppose you want to use a series of commands to open a spreadsheet file and add two percent to every item in column

Digital Dave's Tip

A keyboard overlay, or template, is a real big help when learning a new word processor, spreadsheet or other application. The templates fit around the keys on the keyboard, spotlighting which keys fit the applicaton's commands. This saves a lot of wear and tear on the manual, and speeds up the learning of new commands. If a template did not come with the program, ask for one at your local software shop.

seven, recalculate and close the file. Fine, you just type in the commands for each step.

Further suppose that you need to increase the price in column seven—in 37 separate spreadsheet files. That's a lot of typing of commands. Here comes the macro to the rescue.

You set up a macro with all of the commands you'd type to make the change manually, except the filename would have a special symbol.

Now you would invoke the macro with the name of the first file after it. The macro processor (a piece of your software, not the opposite of a *microprocessor*) would take the filename you typed in and replace that special symbol, then execute all the commands.

Now all you have to do is invoke the macro with each filename and the computer does the rest. Saves a lot of wear and tear on your typing finger.

Digital Dave

Inside PC-DOS

Here's a brief look at some of the software that comes with your IBM PC or clone. It's called PC-DOS, or in some circles MS-DOS, and it's made up of the program that takes care of all the housekeeping chores, and a bunch of utility programs, or tools to do fixup and repair work. Here's an aspect of PC-DOS that's built right in.

Dear Digital Dave,
 What is a BATCH, and where can I learn how to use one?

Mary Banning

Dear Mary,
 BATCH is part of your computer's operating system. It's a simple way of storing keystrokes that you use over and over. It can't do anything you can't do from the keyboard, but it can type a lot faster than you can.
 For instance, before I start up my *Paint* program I like to switch to the Hercules graphics mode. I made up a simple PAINT.BAT file that gives the command to the video adapter to switch modes, and then starts up *Paint*.
 Many INSTALL programs that automate the installation of new programs for you are simply BATCH files that give the commands to create directories and move files from floppies to your hard drive.
 Most books on DOS, or whatever operating system you are using, will have a chapter on the use of BATCH. The book *Power Tools, Techniques, Tricks and Utilities* covers it, along with a lot of other DOS goodies.

Digital Dave

There are many aspects of the operating system that are changing as computers become more user friendly. In the bad old days you dealt with the operating system, such as it was, by feeding in punched cards or paper tape. Most computers today use a text-based interface, and have the cursor blinking at you to indicate where the computer expects the next input. The new graphical interface brings a new concept to the fore.

Dear Digital Dave,
 I've run into the term "hotspot" when reading about cursors. What does it mean?

Cynthia Jordan

Dear Cynthia,

In the old days of character-oriented displays, the cursor pointed to a whole character on the screen, so any sort of blinking blob was adequate. With the new mouse- and graphics-oriented programs made popular by the Macintosh, you are pointing at individual pixels (PIcture ELementS), which are very small.

If the cursor were the same size as the pixels you're trying to point at, it would be so small it would be lost on a screen full of graphics. To solve this problem, a cursor much larger than the thing being pointed at was invented. Only one very small part of the cursor is the active spot, or hotspot. In the case of an arrow, the tip of the arrow is the hotspot. The active portion of a crosshair is where the hairs cross.

Many of the programming languages for the Macintosh support the definition of new cursor shapes, for which you must pinpoint the hotspot.

Digital Dave

Major Software Categories

The first type of software we'll look at is spreadsheets. The spreadsheet program has become popular not only with the green-eyeshade set, but also with engineers, scientists and others who have to do what-if and trade-off studies.

Dear Digital Dave,

I use my PC mostly for word processing. I have a friend who just bought a spreadsheet program and told me it was amazing, yet I can't find any reason why I should have a spreadsheet. I own no business and I do my checking in my checkbook, thank you. What can a spreadsheet do that's so amazing?

Vern Leah

Dear Vern,

Spreadsheets are amazing, and that's why everyone gets excited about them. But you are right, there aren't many really useful things to do with them, unless you do a lot of financial or engineering work.

A spreadsheet program is a big help when doing a "what-if" type calculation, where you are trying to optimize the bottom line. Suppose you have a garden in your back yard that is 10 feet by 10 feet, and you want to plant tomatoes, corn, beans and peas.

You only have $20 to spend on seed and fertilizer. The fertilizer makes the corn grow twice as much, but only helps the other crops by 25 percent. You are trying to decide if you should pay twice as much for the hybrid tomatoes, which have a higher yield, or spend the money on the fertilizer and make all the crops grow more.

This is the kind of problem you can crunch in the spreadsheet, trying many different possibilities. What if you dug up the grass and made the garden twice as big? No sweat for the spreadsheet to recalculate. Now, let's see. Should I buy the extra-lean ground beef at $1.89 or the standard grade at $1.19? My cardiologist raised his rates to $110 per visit, so the bottom line shows that the extra lean is cheaper.

Digital Dave

Many people don't understand the difference between a spreadsheet and a database manager. That's because the programmers of the two types of applications are doing their best to incorporate the features from one into the other.

Dear Digital Dave,

What does the term "database" mean? I've used spreadsheets, but a friend told me to switch to a database because they are more powerful.

Chance Fields

Digital Dave's Tip

Even if you don't have a fancy database manager program, you can make lists of books, records or other household collections, and keep them in order. Use your word processor to maintain the list in alphabetical order. It's easy to insert new entries in their proper location and print a new copy of the list.

Dear Chance,

A spreadsheet, as you have figured out, is like a piece of paper with rows and columns ruled out. You put data and equations into the squares and add formulas that make simple or complex calculations.

A database is an organized list of data. You make up the organization before you put the data into the database. The data can then be reorganized, sorted, added to and deleted from over and over.

Usually a database is made up of records, which are, in turn, made up of fields. For instance, a personnel database would be made up of records, one for each employee, with each record made up of fields such as name, employee number, job title, Social Security number and age.

With one quick command, you could get a report on all vice presidents over 40 years old with an SSN with a first digit greater than five, which would mean they probably were raised on the West Coast.

How about a sorted list of parts in an inventory database? Try to do that with a spreadsheet!

Digital Dave

Suppose you don't have the time or the money to invest in the top-of-the-line application programs, or you have a somewhat limited home computer that's been kicking around the house for too many years. Put it to use, even if you only have a rudimentary text editor.

Dear Digital Dave,
   What's the difference between a word processor and an editor? Aren't they the same thing? What are the differences in word processors/editors? If they differ, can I find a word processor that I can use for both functions?

Fred Post

Dear Fred,
   If you want to write a letter on your computer, an editor only gets you halfway there. The word processor does the whole job. On the other hand, if you are programming, the features of the word processor just get in the way.
   Just as you need a saw to cut up wood, then a hammer to nail the pieces together to build a dog house, an editor lets you add and delete text to a file on your computer, then you need a separate formatter program to take the text file and organize it so the printer can handle it.
   Back in the old days of computers (a few years ago), the editor and the formatter were separate programs that did not work together. Often the commands for the formatter had to be imbedded in the text, which was a real pain, because you couldn't tell what the text would look like until you printed it.
   A word processor combines the editor and formatter in one program, and the formatting commands are hidden in the text file, while the screen looks pretty much the same as the printed page.
   Now what if you are trying to write a program instead of print a pretty page? Well, all those hidden formatting commands come back to haunt you. The output file might make a particular brand of printer happy, but all the commands have to be stripped out before a program compiler can handle it.
   Editors that are written especially for a certain computer language can have some great special features. It gets to be a hassle to indent lines when you are doing structured programming, so some editors have a feature where it will indent every

line until you tell it to quit. Some editors can even do some simple checking of the program syntax to keep you from many of the dumb typing mistakes.

Digital Dave

The ultimate word processor is the desktop publishing program. It handles not only text, but also graphics and pictures. Because these programs are so powerful and versatile, much more support is required in the way of libraries of character fonts and collections of pictures to be cut and pasted into the document being produced.

Add-Ons

The following letter illustrates another gotcha when purchasing software: the costly add-ons. The bottom end of the desktop publishing and CAD software market is full of the cheap come-on, with the list of additions needed to really make it work in fine print on the back of the box.

One way of scoping this out before you buy is to go to a well-stocked software store and look at your prospective purchase on the shelf. Note the number of boxes with similar covers, then pick up those boxes and read what they are good for. You will learn a lot about the add-ons from the boxes.

There are ways to get around this, especially in the area of clip-art and digitized pictures, which are becoming available from low-cost, third-party suppliers. What the heck, they can digitize a whole diskette full of pictures in an hour and sell it to you for a low price and still make a few bucks. It's better than the high-priced spread from the original software supplier. Unfortunately, the CAD market hasn't developed much low-cost third-party support yet.

Dear Digital Dave,
    I purchased a simple desktop publisher program called **First Publisher** *for my PC. It works very well for my purposes, except for graphics. The program came with a few*

interesting graphics files, and more are available from the maker of **First Publisher.** *The problem is that the graphics files cost more than the original program, if you want to buy a bunch of them! I can't afford to shell out for a pile of disks, just to get a few images that I want. What can I do?*

Hans Jergensen

Dear Hans,

I bought a copy of that program for my daughter's new computer for Christmas. I like it too, and I ran into the same problem. The ticket is that *First Publisher*, and I assume most of the rest of the desktop publishing programs on the market, can import images from other sources.

The manual says that you can grab artwork created by *PC Paintbrush*, or even stuff generated on the Macintosh if you can transfer the file to an IBM disk. I haven't had a chance to try out these tricks, but I did run across something interesting.

The picture files on some public domain disks have the same file extension (.MAC) as the *First Publisher* art library. I thought, what the heck, I'll try it. I grabbed a file called BROOKE.MAC, and sure enough it worked!

My daughter's best friend's father was turning 40, so he got a newspaper with the headline "Brooke Shields Goes for Man 40," and a picture of her, all generated on the computer and printed out on a dot matrix printer.

I see a large pool of artwork and scanned photographic images becoming available at very low cost to support the desktop publishing boom. It's just too easy to create the stuff.

Digital Dave

The BASICs of Programming

Okay, we've talked about all those great application programs that let you manipulate words, numbers and pictures to your heart's content. What if there is a task you want to do, and you can't find a program that does it? You have to write a program to do it yourself! To some, writing programs on a computer is the ultimate word puzzle. You thought the hard decisions were over when you bought your computer. That purchase only opened the door to many more forks in the road.

Dear Digital Dave,

I just bought a Commodore 128 computer because I want to learn how to program. I figured it would be fun to learn using the BASIC that comes with the computer.

My son, who is taking computer science courses at UCSD, insists that I should not learn BASIC—that it will ruin me for life, and I should learn PASCAL. Will I be poisoned if I learn BASIC?

Dan Jerold

Dear Dan,

Yes, you'll be ruined if you mess with BASIC. You'll be able to write one-page programs that do some fantastic graphics on the screen. You could sit down and produce a program in one evening that will play a simple game or keep your checkbook, and you'll have fun.

With PASCAL you have to write three pages of code to get your computer to say, "Hi, World!" Forget about graphics. None here.

One the other hand, if you intend to get a job programming for a living, suffer the boredom of PASCAL. It forces the good habits people who write code for a living must have.

Digital Dave

Not only do you have many choices, you can learn whole new languages. At least the words look like English, but the syntax sure is different.

Dear Digital Dave,
   I am somewhat new to writing BASIC programs on my Kaypro PC clone, but I have run into a complete roadblock. I know how to start up BASIC, write and run programs, and start over again with the NEW command, but I don't know how to get back to the DOS prompt without rebooting the computer. I tried QUIT, DONE, BYE and just about every other word I could think of, including a few you shouldn't print. Nothing works. I've looked and looked in my GW BASIC manual. Once I'm in BASIC am I stuck?

Cristeen Burkhouse

Dear Cristeen,
   I guess that back in the old days of BASIC on CP/M machines, things were a lot more simple. There were no commands like CIRCLE and DRAW to clog up the manual. Of course, we couldn't do any graphics on our character-only screens.
   Now that BASIC has about ten million commands, it's easy to miss some of the basic BASIC (sorry, I couldn't resist) commands. The one you are looking for to get you back to the system is SYSTEM. I know, why didn't you think of that?
   I have the same problem when I start learning a new language, and every new application program has a new language. I've been learning a Computer Aided Design (CAD) program to make the drawings of the deck I'm building in the back yard. *EasyCAD* (easy, ha!) has 89 basic commands.
   It has pull-down menus so you can access commands with the mouse instead of typing them in. The only problem is that I end up pulling down every menu twice before I find what I'm looking for. I work with the manual in one hand and the mouse in the other.
   This program has both an END and a QUIT command.

What's the difference? I don't know; I have to look it up. So much for on-screen help.

The biggest help for finding commands is a cheat sheet, like the one that came with my *Leading Edge* Word Processor. It's just a fold-out card with a one-sentence description of all the commands. That's the quickest way to learn all the commands.

Now, where did I put that cheat sheet?

Digital Dave

BASIC was designed to teach students how to program, not to be a programming language. Later, as microprocessors became more popular, software developers started tacking on all the usual things that come with a real language, like being able to calculate large numbers. Even in this day of the high-powered Macintosh, the process of refining the language has not stopped.

Dear Digital Dave,
Why are there two different versions of the Microsoft BASIC for the Macintosh? Which one should I buy?
Henry Ichan

Dear Henry,

I guess the people at Microsoft couldn't decide which was most important, being right or being first. One version of BASIC for the Mac processes numbers in decimal format, just like we do, so it will get the same answers you would get counting on your fingers.

The answers will agree, right down to the last penny. All this finger counting slows things up, so another version of BASIC is provided. This one uses the full power of the 68000 microprocessor to do 32-bit binary calculations.

This goes much faster, but sometimes rounding-off errors can creep in. Not to say the answers are wrong, they just don't agree with the way you would do it using decimal math.

Don't worry, you get both versions of BASIC for one low price, but you have to decide which one to use.

Digital Dave

Copy Protection

Here's a big black mark on the software industry. What other product do you know of that is purposefully damaged by the manufacturer?

Dear Digital Dave,
I bought a program labeled "Copy Protected" the other day. Now I hear I really shouldn't have purchased it. Did I make a mistake?

Dan Klowden

Dear Dan,
Copy protection is a pain in the disk drive, but it can save you some money. It depends on the type of program and the method of copy protection.

Most protection schemes depend on screwing up the disk in some way so that copy programs can't duplicate the disk. Some schemes add an additional track, or a different number of sectors than is standard. Some even resort to such things as putting bad sectors on the disk by burning specific spots with a laser!

If you are into games, would you rather pay $19.95 for a copy-protected game disk, or $59.95 for an unprotected version because the manufacturer figures every unprotected disk he sells will be copied by at least two people? I would buy the cheaper one, and be real careful that my dog doesn't chew up the only copy.

Now if you were buying a database manager program that you'd use to keep track of your inventory in your store, would you want to depend on a floppy disk that the manufacturer purposefully screwed up? No way!

So you see, there are a lot of angles to the copy-protection question. Many manufacturers of software are just now figuring out the marketplace.

Digital Dave

Summary

Software is the gasoline that runs the engine of your computer. You can sit in the driver's seat all you want, but you don't go anywhere without software! The cost of an application program is not just the hit your VISA card takes in the computer shop when you pick out that spreadsheet or database manager. You have to invest a lot of midnight oil to become a power user.

Just as computer hardware has become more powerful and more similar, the major application programs have grown and absorbed each others' features so that the differences are disappearing. The user interface on many programs has been improved to the point where a few minutes of fooling around will enable you to use the basic functions of the program. The "but" is that the features of the program have multiplied to the point that you will have to plow through a 500-page manual to learn what else the program can do.

PART II

CHAPTER 4

Disks and Disk Drives

We talked about what software did for us in detail in the last chapter. Well, now that we have it, where are we going to keep it? All those software instructions disappear from the RAM when you shut the power off. Besides, we don't have nearly enough RAM to hold all the programs and data we have on hand. The disk drive takes care of this program and data storage when the lights are out.

Back in the old days of computers, everybody used magnetic tape to record data. In movies from the 1950s, the computer was depicted as a large tape deck, with the reels spinning back and forth rapidly. That's not really the computer—only the tape storage.

Tape storage is still on the computer scene, though it's usually some sort of tape cartridge instead of open reels. It's good for backing up data that doesn't need to be accessed very often. The drawback of tape is that it takes so long to retrieve a specific piece of data. If the data happens to be on the other end of the tape, you have to wait for the tape deck to wind the tape from one reel to the other to find the data. That takes a lot of time!

The engineers at IBM wanted to create a storage medium that accessed the data quickly, but was inexpensive and simple to operate. The next letter finishes this history.

Dear Digital Dave,
    Why are hard drives called hard drives, and why are floppy disks called floppies?

                                            Karen Sumner

Dear Karen,
    Back in the old days, there were only hard drives, a flat piece of aluminum with magnetic material coated on each side. Then they were just called disk drives, because it was a flat disk. Disk drives were complex mechanical things with precise alignment, so they were very expensive. IBM started developing a gadget for loading small amounts of data for housekeeping chores on their mainframes.
    The IBM engineers took a piece of magnetic recording tape, before it was cut up into the thin pieces we use in cassette recorders, and punched out a round disk, about eight inches in diameter. They put this disk in a plastic envelope and built an inexpensive drive to read and write to it. The drive design took advantage of the flexible disk to ease up on the precision alignment required. Thus was born the floppy diskette.
    Since then, the diskettes have been downsized to 5¼ inches and 3½ inches, which are a lot easier to handle. Since the flexible diskettes are floppies, we had to call the original disks something to differentiate them, so they became hard disks. Not because they are hard to use, but because the disk itself is not flexible.

                                            Digital Dave

Digital Dave's Tip

You've all read the warnings about keeping magnets away from your floppy disks. If you have an old-style desk telephone with a real bell in it, keep it away from your disks, too. That ringer puts out a humdinger of a magnetic field. Better yet, put that phone somewhere else in the house and use a telephone with an electronic ringer.

Protecting Your Disk Drives and Data

One aspect of the floppy diskette is the write-protect notch, which helps protect against accidental erasure of your data. The new 3½-inch micro diskettes have a solid plastic jacket, so its write-protect notch has been redesigned.

Dear Digital Dave,
I have a new Macintosh that uses the dinky plastic diskettes. There is a little window in the corner with a shade, which is supposed to have something to do with "write protecting" the diskette. How does this work? Is it the same on the IBM PS/2 diskettes?

Helen Jones

Dear Helen,
That little window is open or closed to let light from an LED strike a phototransistor, which gives the disk drive a go or no-go for writing data to the diskette. When it's closed, the drive will write data normally. When it's open to let light through, the drive will refuse to write.

If you have a master diskette of a program or some important data that you don't want to lose, I would open the window, so the computer cannot overwrite the program or data. Make a copy of the diskette to work with, just in case.

Since this window controls circuitry that's right in your disk drive, the mechanism will work the same if the drive is installed in a Mac, a PC or a PS/2.

Digital Dave

Digital Dave's Tip

Don't lay floppy disks down without their protective envelope. They generate static electricity when they spin, so they suck up all the dust off your table top if you lay them down unprotected. Put the floppy back in the envelope whenever it's not in the drive.

Back at the beginning of the chapter we talked about how the
write-protect shutter on the new microfloppy diskettes worked. The
old-style 5¼-inch minifloppy just has a notch cut in the side of the
jacket for the same purpose. To write-protect it, you have to stick an
adhesive tab over the notch.

Dear Digital Dave,
   Okay, Dave, here's one for you: write-protect tabs. I get
a sheet of about two dozen of them with every box of disks
I buy. I say, "Why bother?" Half of them don't stick, and
even then, I wind up un-tabbing the disks because I need to
write to the disk again. Is there a better way to write-protect
a disk?

                                             Larry Kreyszig

Dear Larry,
   It sounds like you are doing a bit of over write-protecting.
Then the process gets in the way of having fun with your
computer. The write-protect tabs are to protect from writing
to a disk that has valuable data on it that you don't intend to
change.
   The last part is the key: data that you don't intend to
change. For instance, when I purchase a new program, or
download it from a bulletin board, I make sure I have all the
pieces (document files, READ.ME files and so on) on one
disk. Then I put a write-protect tab on it, make a working copy
and store the write-protected master disk away.
   One trick to sticking on the write-protect tab is to put it on
so that only enough of the tab is wrapped around the back to
cover up the notch. If you leave too much to wrap around the
back, it ends up with a gap where it goes from the folded-over
piece of the disk jacket to the back. It always seems to peel
off that way.
   Yes, there is a better way to write-protect a disk, and the
people who designed the 3½-inch microfloppy found it. They

put a small plastic tab that slides back and forth in a slot. One position is write-protect and the other is normal. It's reusable, and it won't peel off!

Digital Dave

Diskettes come in all price ranges, from the low-priced, bulk-packed, no-name mail-order specials, to the name brands with fancy packages, and fancy prices.

Dear Digital Dave,
I have been purchasing diskettes for a very low price via mail-order, but when I format them, some of the floppies show several thousand bytes as being bad. Is there something wrong with these diskettes? Should I use them if they have bad bytes?

Samantha Driva

Dear Sam,
In the bad old days, there were cheap disks (bad) and expensive disks (usually good). Then the quality of all the disk manufacturers improved to the point where all the floppy diskettes were pretty good, or so I thought.

I just received a shipment of those four-for-a-buck (if you buy 100) diskettes. I went through and formatted the first 25, and about a half dozen went right in the trash can.

They looked fine, and they ran quiet in the drive, which is usually a sign of a well-made diskette, but 20 percent of them had hard errors. Even if I reformatted them, they still had errors. This makes me leery of using any of the batch, and like I said, the ones with errors are now lining my out file.

If these clowns are going to sell untested diskettes for a very low price, fine. I can sort out the few bad ones and throw them away. But the advertisement (I went back and read it again) said that all of the disks are 100-percent checked. Maybe they don't reject the bad ones, they just test them.

Anyway, the only thing I intend to use them for is to give away copies of public domain software (I've got a bunch), to friends (I also have a bunch), and I'm cheap. None of my critical files will ever come near those *el cheapo* floppies.

Digital Dave

One way of protecting against data loss is to make copies of the data on another floppy diskette, which then gets put away in a safe place. This is called "backing up" data. A problem arises when you have a large hard drive with large data files. It can take a long time to back up when your hard drive can hold 60 floppies worth of data!

Dear Digital Dave,
   Backing up is a pain in the you-know-where. Is there any way I can do regular backups without taking two hours out of my daily routine?

Jessica Weis

Dear Jessica,
   If you are like most users, most of the data from your hard disk that you need to back up hasn't changed since you loaded it. For instance, your word processor and spreadsheet programs don't change. Back them up on separate diskettes and label them clearly.
   The only thing that changes is your data, whether it's a letter to a customer or a spreadsheet file, so you really only need to back up the files that get changed. Keeping records of which files have been updated can reduce the chore.
   If you keep your clock set to the right date and time, either with a hardware clock or by religiously setting it every time you boot, you can use the date and time when you do a DIRectory. That's why the dates and times are there.
   If you use the BACKUP and RESTORE commands, all of this sorting of files to find only those that have changed

Digital Dave's Tip

Protect those store-bought programs you paid so much for. Go out and buy yourself a floppy disk tray with a locking lid. Put all, and I mean all of your original disks in it, lock it, and put it where the kids can't get their sticky fingers on it, and where you won't be tempted to grab an original in the middle of a panic. Instead, use the backup copies you keep in the tray on your desk.

since that last backup is automatic. One warning: This only works if the date and time are accurate!

Of course, a tape backup unit is the ultimate. They cost from $300 to $700, but they are the only way to go if you have large databases to maintain.

Digital Dave

Floppy Disk Dos and Don'ts

Since the data that your floppy diskettes hold is probably the most valuable part of your computer setup, here are some tips to help you protect those diskettes.

The data is stored on your floppies as tiny magnetic domains. The material on the disk is really just very finely ground iron. The write head in the drive magnetizes the iron particles one way or the other to indicate ones or zeros. A magnetic field from any source can wipe out your precious data.

Magnets and dust are not the only hazards to your diskettes. The ballpoint pen can wipe one out in a hurry. Use only a Flair type pen on a label that has already been attached to a floppy.

Dear Digital Dave,

Why can't we use a pen to label our floppy disks? At my office, whenever I take up a pen to label my files everybody within 20 feet gasps and genuflects (not necessarily in that order), and 30 felt-tip pens are thrust my way.

Are my co-workers merely sheep, superstitiously follow-ing the herd, or is there an actual, factual basis for their fervent obedience?

Dianne Brefnan

Dear Di,

You don't believe, huh? Well try this little experiment. Take a brand new floppy disk. Stick it in your computer and go through the formatting routine. This should give you a perfect disk, ready for data.

Now stick a label on it and write in large letters the word TRASH on the label with a ballpoint pen. Press firmly so you get nice bold strokes.

Now stick it back in the computer and format the disk again. Not so good this time? You just kissed off a disk.

The pressure from the sharp point of the ball point pen leaves dents in the disk material, which makes the head bounce when it goes over the dents, which does a number on your data.

All of the above applies to the 8- or 5¼-inch floppy disks.

Digital Dave's Tip

You can't afford a hard drive, so you leave your boot diskette in the drive all the time. That way you won't loose it.

Or your favorite game needs the original floppy in drive A to run, so you just leave it there.

Not a good idea. Most floppy drives these days don't pull the heads off the disk unless the drive door is open. That means there is constant pressure on the diskette at the spot where the heads come to rest. Eventually it's going to cause a problem.

Also, moisture and dust will tend to collect where the head sits, and the last thing you need is moisture or dust stuck on your head. No, no! The head in your disk drive, not the one that's nominally on your shoulders.

> If you are working with the new 3½-inch disks with the hard
> shell, go bah-bah to the flock in the office and write away
> with your ballpoint.
>
> *Digital Dave*

Over the course of the short history of the floppy diskette there have
been many false representations by the manufacturers, and many
hackers who have delighted in taking advantage of these quirks to
get more for their money. One example is the differentiation diskette
manufacturers made between single-sided and double-sided 5¼-
inch diskettes. The single-sided naturally sold for less.

The trouble is, there is no such thing as a single-sided floppy. All
of them have the magnetic coating on both sides, hence can be used
in a double-sided drive. Some people even used both sides on a
single-sided drive by punching another hole in the diskette jacket so
they could flip the diskette over and use the other side. No wonder
users were skeptical when the high-density diskettes came out. More
of the old "slap a new label on it and raise the price" trick?

Dear Digital Dave,

*In one of your tips you state, "You cannot and should
not try to use a high-density diskette in a 360K drive; it won't
work." Common sense says that any medium that will work
at a high-bit density should work at a lower-bit density. So
please, why won't it work?*

Cecil H. Royce

Digital Dave's Tip

*Keeping track of all those floppies laying around is a pain. Even
if you are the neat type and file your diskettes in a nice floppy file
cabinet, how do you spot the ones you want right away?*

*Buy yourself a pack of colored diskettes. Make your boot disk blue,
your games orange, your spreadsheet green, and you will never have
to flip through your whole disk file again.*

Dear Cecil,

Back in the old days, the diskette manufacturers thought they had us fooled with the higher prices of double-sided diskettes over the single-sided version, when in fact all diskettes were double-sided. You think they pulled the same sort of trick this time?

Well, they got smarter. High-density diskettes are different from the regular ones. The magnetic properties of the coating (you know, the stuff that holds the bits) are different. Regular diskettes have a magnetic coercivity of 320 oysters (or Oersteds, or something like that), where the high-density model boasts 640 of those babies.

You might get the expensive floppies to work in your economy drive, but it won't be as reliable as the plain old low-octane diskette it was designed for.

Digital Dave

Protecting Your Hard Drive

In most hard drives, the head is removed from the disk when the power is turned off. On the older hard drives you should use a program like Seek Inside Track (SIT) or PARK to put the head somewhere that won't cause a problem when you knock off for the night. On most floppy drives, that head just sits on the disk all the time.

For those of you who are too lazy to type SIT or PARK just before you shut down your computer, or just don't trust your memory, the following question indicates a way out.

Digital Dave's Tip

If you listen to loud music with high-powered headphones, like I do, when you compute, keep those headphones away from your diskettes! The headphones have powerful magnets in them, which will damage the data on the diskettes. I try to keep the headphones in the rack with the stereo, and not on the desk with the diskettes.

Dear Digital Dave,
   I read in your column about a program called SAFEPARK that automatically parked the heads of your hard drive. Where can I get a copy of that program? That will take the worry out of letting my son use my PC.
                                                      Paul Descarties

Dear Paul,
   The SAFEPARK program sounds like something you'd find in the public domain, but I haven't found a program like it available. SAFEPARK comes with *Disk Technician Plus*, a program that cleans up your hard disk for you.
   Apparently, SAFEPARK only works with *Disk Technician Plus*, because the *Disk Technician* program creates the safe zone where the heads land after SAFEPARK moves them there automatically. If somebody gives you a copy of SAFEPARK, don't use it!
   Stick with SIT (Seek Inside Track), or the PARK programs that you have to run manually, or go out and buy *Disk Technician Plus*. It's only about $60 or $70 at the discount price, and it can (and will, but you won't know it) save you from 10 times that amount of frustration when you have a hard drive problem due to track misalignment.
                                                      Digital Dave

For some reason, way back when, somebody decided that disk drives work better oriented one way or the other. Unfortunately, one somebody claimed that vertical was the right way, and another somebody went for horizontal.

Dear Digital Dave,
   I have heard mixed information about placing a CPU on its side. I have heard that in this position the life of the disk drives can be greatly shortened. I've also heard just the opposite—that it really doesn't harm the unit at all.

What's the real truth? Does it harm the CPU to be placed on its side?

Richard Olney

Dear Richard,

By "a CPU on its side," I assume that you mean placing the system unit upright on the floor. I have my AT on the left side of my desk and the '386 on the right, both on their side on the floor.

I picked a desk with a large overhang, specifically to leave room for an upright computer system unit. I never dreamed I would need both sides of the desk for this purpose.

There is a file cabinet on one side and a stereo rack on the other. The point of all this is that the computer unit is protected on all sides from abuse—one of the reasons not to put a computer on the floor.

As far as the sideways position causing a problem with the disk drives, I don't see a problem. There might be one or two drives on the market that wouldn't work well in that position, but they would have to be a very poor design prone to failure in any position.

I've checked the manufacturer's literature on a few disk drives, and all of them claim that vertical or horizontal mounting is okay. Hard drives are a lot more rugged than they were in the old days. We're finding them in portable computers that put up with more stress than setting a system unit on its side would ever induce.

Digital Dave

Your Floppy Disk Drives

Back in the days of PCs equipped with 128K of RAM and no hard drive, everybody had two floppy drives. One was used to boot up and run programs, while the other was used for storing data. These days, the need for two floppies of the same size has dwindled.

Dear Digital Dave,

How many disk drives should I get with my PC? I have one floppy drive and one hard disk. Should I buy another floppy?

Dennis Fraggy

Dear Dennis,

When I ordered my PC, I only asked for one floppy drive, but the salesman threw in a second one because he was such

Digital Dave's Tip

Don't drink and (floppy) drive. One spill will make a mess of your data. If you insist on drinking anything, even water, near your computer, find a shelf lower than your desktop to put your glass on. That way the mess will only be on the floor. I've found that those sports bottles with the covered top are great for keeping spills away from my computer and floppy disks. Still, I keep the bottle on the floor.

SR

a nice guy. I was trying to save a buck, but I am glad he gave me the second drive.

Now, the only thing I use the second floppy drive for is to copy floppies, but I do that a whole lot. It's especially useful when copying old PC-DOS 1.1 single-sided public domain disks to double-sided 360K disks.

If you want to copy a floppy with only one drive, you'd better have at least 512K of RAM. Otherwise you have to switch disks a bunch.

Digital Dave

Everybody is jumping on the bandwagon to move to the new microfloppy diskettes. If you have a library of 5¼-inch diskettes, you'll want to keep at least one of your old drives.

Dear Digital Dave,
    I own a PC-XT clone and would like to install a 3½-inch disk drive for convenience. I was told by a computer dealer that I would need to install a new BIOS in the computer to be able to operate the drive.
    I believe he mentioned that I needed to have PHOENIX BIOS 3.XX or higher. Is this true? Also, am I going to have to purchase a special controller for the drive? If I do have to have an updated BIOS, is this as simple as going down to the local computer dealer and buying the 2764 and 27256 ROM to replace on the motherboard. Can it be this simple?
    Joe Sadony

Dear Joe,
    Actually, it's simpler than that. Santa Claus brought my daughter a laptop computer that uses the 3½-inch drives, so naturally I had to put one of those dinky drives in my machine so we could swap data.
    The kit came with an adapter frame that made the micro-floppy drive fit the 5¼-inch drive hole in my big old clunky

desktop machine. The kit also adapted the connectors so I could use the cables already in my computer.

After removing the cover, I unplugged the two connectors on the back of my B drive, took out two screws, and out came the old drive. Two screws and two connectors later, the new drive was hooked up and ready to go.

The only software change was an upgrade to DOS 3.2. My machine is a rather old clone with a no-name floppy controller. I stuck the new DOS disk in, booted up, and the microfloppy worked on the first try! Boy, was I surprised. I'm used to having a struggle every time I install a new piece of hardware.

I haven't heard of any floppy controllers or BIOS ROMs that must be replaced before you can add a 760K microfloppy drive. With 1.44MB drives, many of the older PCs do need the BIOS chips upgraded.

Digital Dave

Dear Digital Dave,

I have an XT clone with two 5¼-inch, 360K drives. Now I want to replace one of the 5¼-inch drives with a 3½-inch, 720K drive. However, I would like the 3½-inch drive to be drive A and boot the system from it. Is it possible to do that, or does the 3½-inch drive only work as drive B?

Jim

Dear Jim,

Remember that you need at least PC-DOS version 3.2 to use the 3½-inch drives, and that you need to make a 3½-inch

---

Digital Dave's Tip

Yes, I know those cute little 3½-inch microfloppies fit in a shirt pocket, but don't do it! The shutter is to keep big things, like fingerprints, out. Dust can still sneak in. Keep them in a protective case.

disk with DOS on it before installing the drive as the boot drive. I would install the new drive as B to start out. Format a 3½-inch floppy and transfer DOS to it with the SYSTEM command.

Also copy the *.SYS files over. Now swap the cables around to make the 3½-inch drive your A drive, and reboot.

Digital Dave

Disk Problems

Now let's look at some disk problems and how to correct them.

Dear Digital Dave,

I need help badly. I have had my Commodore 1541 disk drive aligned five times since February, and it's out of whack again!

I took it to a local computer outlet to get it aligned in order to use Multiplan, *the spreadsheet. After two alignments, it still wouldn't run. I gave up on the spreadsheet and stuck with* WordPro 3 Plus/64.

After a third alignment, Multiplan *worked, but only until May. I got it realigned again, and it has worked one week and now is out again. It always says "file not found error" and flashes red. It won't run the Commodore test disk, either.*

My computer is only 1 year old; I don't use it daily, and the only program I really use is WordPro 3 Plus/64. *Am I*

Digital Dave's Tip

When finishing up with your word processor, always wait for the disk drive light to go out and the DOS prompt to appear on the screen before pulling out the floppy disk. With many programs, pulling out the floppy too soon will cause a loss of data, possibly an entire file.

crazy, or jinxed, or do I need to spend $40 somewhere else for better-quality work? Please help.

Don Rutkoff

Dear Don,

That's not a very encouraging situation, is it? But it shouldn't be too hard to troubleshoot, if we just put on our thinking caps. Let's do a few experiments to eliminate some possible problems.

If the disks themselves were bad they wouldn't work on a properly aligned drive. Try your disks on another machine. Did you trash them by putting them too close to an electric motor or transformer? Okay, so the disks work fine on your buddy's C-64.

If the drives were out of alignment, then they will work fine, as long as they are trying to read data written by the misaligned heads. Use BASIC to write some files. Can you read them back? If you can, then you have an alignment problem.

If you can't read the files you just wrote, there is an electrical problem, such as a chip that is going West. Take it in to get repaired by people who know what they're doing.

Assuming you can read what you just wrote, but older disks are unreadable, your heads are out of alignment. If the tech at the computer store couldn't get it right after five tries, then find another tech, and another store.

Digital Dave

As I mentioned, the Macintosh is designed to protect you from yourself, and from screwing up your data, by keeping you from pulling the floppy out of the drive before the computer is done with it. The designers did this by building an automatic diskette ejector into the drive that will only spit out the diskette on command from the computer. Sometimes this doesn't work out.

Dear Digital Dave,
*   I own a Macintosh and an external floppy disk drive.*
One of the disks got stuck in the external drive. How do I
get it out? Help!

*   Gary Putnam*

Dear Gary,
    Be thankful that it was the external drive, and haul it off
to the fix-it shop. They will have to take the drive apart to get
it out, so you might have to do without for a day or two.
    I know there are ways to pry the disk out by sticking a
paper clip in, but there is a good chance that you will trash
one of the heads, since they are probably still in contact with
the disk instead of being retracted for disk removal.
    Using old, dirty diskettes and sticking more than one label
on are the usual causes of this problem. Always peel off the
old label before putting on a new one.

*   Digital Dave*

Whose Lifetime?

    Did you ever wonder if a lifetime warranty was for *your* life span,
or if it just covered the product until you got it home, which is the
lifetime of the product as far as the manufacturer is concerned?

Dear Digital Dave,
*   Over the years, I have acquired a number of "bad" disks*
(the "never throw out anything" syndrome).
*   The dealers from whom I've purchased these disks won't*
take them back individually, or else the stores no longer
exist.
*   I don't want my money back (I don't know how much I*
paid for them), but I would like replacement disks. What is
the procedure for getting these disks replaced?

*   Arthur Hard*

Dear Arthur,

I rummaged through my pile of diskettes looking for information about the "lifetime warranty" most diskette manufacturers provide. I did find three boxes of blank disks I didn't know I had, but I only found one warranty, and that was in a box of Sony 3½-inch, high-density floppies.

Anyway, the warranty was spelled out on a slip of paper inside the box. There was a lot of bold-faced fine print protecting Sony from lawsuits, but not one word on how to get a broken diskette fixed or replaced. It did say, "Such replacement shall be the sole remedy of the purchaser."

It looks like the thing to do is stick those bad floppies in an envelope and mail them back to the manufacturer with a nice note about how you like their product, but in this one case you received a faulty product, and that you would live happily ever after if they lived up to their "lifetime warranty."

The big companies depend on customers not taking the time to send a 25-cent disk (with a 25-cent stamp) back to them. They might be so surprised that they'll send you a whole box. At least Sony included their address. Does anyone out there have the address for the White Box Floppy Company? I've got a whole bunch of them to get replaced.

Digital Dave

Digital Dave's Tip

What do you do with those Macintosh disks that bomb when you stick them in the drive? You've already given up hope of recovering the data that was on them, but the disk is probably still good. It just needs to be reformatted, which Apple calls initializing.

Hold down the Option, Tab and Command keys while inserting the disk in the drive. You should get a dialog box, just like you would with a brand-new disk.

Make the same selections as if the diskette just came out of the box and you should have a newly initialized and usable disk in a few moments.

Noisy Disk Drives

Most people think of a computer as the strong silent type, being all electronic. The whoosh of the fan should be all that gives it away, right? Those same people are surprised when they hear the bump and grind of all that mechanical stuff in their new computer. They shouldn't be. After all, most computers have more motors in them than microprocessors.

Dear Digital Dave,

I'm having some trouble with my floppy disk drive on my XT clone. When I use it normally, it makes a few small noises, which I assume is okay. When I format new disks, just before it tells how many bytes are good, or once in a while when I boot up, it makes a grinding noise, even if there is no floppy disk in the drive.

I took it back to the store where I'd purchased it and left it overnight. They said they couldn't find anything wrong with it. This is supposed to be a precision piece of equipment (though the price was right), and I'm afraid it's going to break right after the warranty gives out. Am I being given the runaround?

Gertrude Steiner

Dear Gertrude,

You aren't being given a runaround. Your floppy drive is fine. Some drives are just noisier than others.

The motor that moves the head back and forth across the disk is what's called a stepper motor. It doesn't run smoothly like a regular motor, but jerks from one position to another. And that's exactly what it's supposed to do. It holds the head over one of the tracks, then snaps it in position over the next track.

When the FORMAT program has completed all of the tracks, the head is positioned all the way on the inside of the disk. The computer must move the head back to the home position at the outside track, so it steps the head through all 40 or 80 tracks. Sometimes when you boot up, the head was left near the inside, and again the head is stepped all the way across the disk. This is what makes that grinding sound. The sheet metal on some inexpensive computers tends to amplify the noise and make it seem like the computer is wrenching its guts out, but it's really just doing what it's supposed to do. My floppy disk drives only seem quiet because my Maxtor hard drive is such a screamer.

Digital Dave

Hello, Digital Dave,
I would like to know how to stop my disk drive from squeaking so much. Is there something that I have to lubricate (the drive rod, maybe?).

Virinchi Duvvuri

Dear Viri,
The obvious answer to a squeaking disk drive is to turn the stereo up louder. That solved the bad wheel bearing on my van, until the wheel fell off.

But seriously folks, don't go squirting oil around the insides of your computer. The components were designed to work without additional lubrication. If any oil or grease should get on the disk or the head, major damage to your data would result.

Try turning the disk on its side. This often works with hard disks, too. If it still squeaks, take it in to the shop for repair: You are about to lose your valuable data!

Digital Dave

Summary

Disk drives are the among the most expensive and mechanically complex components of your computer. They deserve respect, and will pay you back with years of reliable data storage. On the other hand, just a bit of abuse from you on a bad day, or from someone else, can spell the end of your invaluable collection of data. Back up or die!

CHAPTER 5

Video Displays

That big eye staring back at you from your computer desk is the subject of today's lecture, so here we go, kiddies. Back in the beginning of this beginner's book, we struggled through the alphabetic mishmash that describes the IBM PC video display adapter cards. I promised you I'd get around to telling you what VGA really stands for. You can make a few bucks on bets with your friends over this one.

Dear Digital Dave,

I know you have been asked this question a million times, but I am new to computers and haven't seen the answer anywhere. Besides, I'd like to see my name in print.

What do the letters VGA stand for? I've been told that Video Graphics Adapter is not the real meaning.

Peggy Keithley

Dear Peggy,

Peggy, Peggy, Peggy. There, that should satisfy your thirst for ink for a while. You are right. VGA does not stand for anything with adapter on the end.

Actually it is the name of an integrated circuit (those chip things that make computers work). During the development stage of the new IBM computers called PS/2s, they designed an upgrade to the EGA, for which they used a gate-array chip. They called it the Video Gate Array, or VGA. The acronym got attached to video adapter cards that emulated the VGA.

A gate-array chip uses a bunch of logic gates that are standard, which are then interconnected in a way that is unique for that application. In other words, it's like taking a standard circuit board full of simple integrated circuits, then hand-wiring them up in a special way to make the logic do what you want.

It's strange that most VGA cards these days are implemented with full, custom-integrated circuits, where each part of the chip is designed from the ground up.

Digital Dave

Monochrome Monitors

Enough fooling around; let's get down to learning about video displays. Most of the IBM line of displays and adapters are compatible with most software, but some incompatibilities exist. The biggest one is that some adapters will not do any kind of graphics. This means a program that only runs in a graphics mode won't work on the non-graphics-equipped computer. That's pretty easy to figure out.

There is one monochrome (black and white) adapter card which didn't come from IBM. Even though it can do great graphics, there are many programs out there it won't work with.

Dear Digital Dave,
I bought a game for my IBM PC the other day, and it doesn't work. In fact, I can't see diddly on the screen. I have a real IBM PC-XT with a Hayes modem, Hercules graphics card and monochrome monitor. Any hints?
Paula Schallum

Dear Paula,

The game was probably working fine, but all the bits that represent the graphics the program worked so hard to manufacture are falling into that bit bucket every computer has. Chances are, your program uses graphics, which means it's expecting a Color Graphics Adapter (CGA). When you bought your computer, I'll bet the computer huckster told you all about the high-resolution graphics of the Hercules card, and you thought all you gave up was pretty colors. Well, he fooled you. He figures you will be back to buy a CGA and a color monitor the first time you try to run a hot game program.

Well, we can fool him back!

There is a public domain program called *SIMCGA* that can put your game and your monochrome graphics adapter on speaking terms. It grabs those bits that were headed for the non-existent CGA, and massages them around so they show up on the monochrome monitor.

I bought a program called *Algebra Plus-1* for my daughter, and *SIMCGA* was provided on the disk for people with just your problem. Check with your friends at the local PC users group, or on your favorite bulletin board, since you have a modem, for a copy of *SIMCGA*.

Digital Dave

While we're on the subject of monochrome monitors, I know there are those of you out there who are on a very tight budget, and are willing to give up color graphics to have a computer at all.

Black and white, or black and green, or black and amber monitors are very easy on the eyes and the pocketbook. The clone Hercules monochrome graphics cards don't work with all software, especially games, but they can be had for less than the cost of a dinner out for you and your loved one.

Dear Digital Dave,
Do you know of an excellent 14-inch monochrome monitor? I have looked at just about every one on the market and found them all unsatisfactory.

Guy Buchanan

Dear Guy,
After staring at a whole bunch of monochrome monitors over the years, even the most expensive ones of 10 years ago were very hard on your eyes compared to some of the very inexpensive monitors available now. That's not to say there isn't some real junk on the market, but some of the hundred-dollar gems sport flat-face tubes with very good linearity and contrast.

If all the monitors look bad to you, I suspect the problem is not the monitor, but the video circuitry in your computer. For instance, if you are hooking up a composite monochrome monitor to a computer that generates color displays, the bandwidth of the signal is limited to make room for the color signals.

The monochrome monitor ignores the color signals, but the bandwidth limits in the computer make the edges of the characters very fuzzy. There isn't anything the monitor can do to fix that. Most home computers that can use a television set for a monitor have this problem. There are modification kits available for most computers to provide a monochrome signal without the bandwidth-limited output. Believe me, it makes a big difference on the monitor screen.

If you're working with an IBM PC or clone, maybe trying a different display adapter will solve your problem. For instance, the character set used on the true-blue IBM Color Graphics Adapter stinks. There just aren't enough dots to make up the character.

I use an ATI card in my clone, which emulates the CGA, but has a chunkier character set with more dots. I usually lean back in my chair, and even on my *el-cheapo* monitor the characters look great from five feet. You have to get within a foot to even see any roughness in the edges of the characters. It's very easy on the eyes and very readable.

Digital Dave

Color Monitors

Okay, so you aren't willing to give up color graphics. You want to see the blue sky in *Flight Simulator*, and the red storm rising in that submarine game. But money doesn't grow on trees, unless you're an avocado farmer.

Dear Digital Dave,
I have an IBM PC computer at home (MAXAR 88T) with a Star nx-1000 Multi-font printer. What do I need to buy to upgrade my computer for more color graphics capabilities in games, etc.?
I know I need a color graphics card and monitor. But which one is best for home use? Also, what else do I need for good color graphics capabilities?

Shawnee Benton

Dear Shawnee,
I know you're going to say I have champagne tastes when you only want me to recommend a beer, but I say go buy a VGA display and card (but check out the prices first). I can walk into most stores and buy a VGA monitor for less money (not even counting inflation) than what I spent for a CGA only a few years ago.

There is so much competition in this area that prices have gone through the floor. You need a VGA card that is compatible with your 8-bit PC bus in your computer, so that cuts you off from the highest-priced cards right there.

First thing to do is check out the ads for VGA monitors

and cards, and combination deals. Then hike down to the store with what looks like the best deal and eyeball the product.

I could talk about dot pitch and lines of resolution here, but in the bottom end of the VGA market, they all have pretty much the same specifications. There are differences in what they look like, but the only way to determine which is best for you is to go look at them.

One way of screwing up a color display is to turn up the brightness too far. It really takes the detail out of the picture. Try to have all the monitors at the same brightness level when you compare them.

A few demonstration programs are around that show off the features of various software packages. They're great for testing the VGA hardware. Try to do the comparisons with the same software demo on each monitor and card you're considering buying. If the store won't demo the hardware, find a different store.

Digital Dave

Let's move up a notch to the top end of the VGA crowd.

Dear Digital Dave,
I would like to have my computer display photographic-quality pictures. Some displays can show very high resolution (1024 by 768), but only 16 colors. Others have lower resolution, but 256 colors. What gives the best picture quality: higher resolution or more colors?

Bonnie Quaid

Dear Bonnie,

In general, your display will look more life-like with more colors. An 800 by 600 display in 256 colors can look so close to a color photo, you can't tell the difference from 3 feet.

Sixteen colors in super-duper resolution does not look good at all when showing a photographic scene. On the other hand, graphics such as charts and graphs look great, and more shades would actually detract. When you buy a new tube to display your pictures, you'll have to get one with analog input. The digital displays can only give you 16 colors. The analog displays are limited in colors only by what your display adapter can put out.

Digital Dave

I used to rail against color monitors because they were so expensive and so hard on the eyes. All that has changed. The text mode of the CGA used to be so bad that I stayed away from color tubes until recently. Now I wouldn't do without.

Dear *Digital Dave*,
In the past you've said that color monitors had poor image quality, and that for text processing a monochrome monitor was better. Is that still true?

Mary Darling

Dear Mary,
It's changed a whole bunch. Many VGA monitors on the market have an image quality just as good as a standard 80-by 25-character monochrome monitor. That's not to say the color tubes come anywhere close to the super-duper, white-on-black screens made especially for desktop publishing.

Standard VGA resolution is a bit better than EGA, which I thought was still substandard, but monitors capable of displaying the SuperVGA resolutions like 1024 by 768 have to use dots of color on the screen so small you can't see them from a normal viewing distance. In fact, I have a hard time seeing them with my face plastered on the screen.

A graphical interface has finally come to the PC, which means that text-based monitors, even for word processing, are going by the wayside.

Digital Dave

Computer Room Setup

That fancy monitor took a big chunk out of your computer budget. A few simple habits will keep it going for years.

One way to keep that monitor safe and healthy is to make sure it's in a safe environment. With all the concern about product safety these days, is there anything to watch out for in your computer room?

Dear Digital Dave,
How safe is it to use our Commodore 64 with our TV set?
Hans Jerimain

Dear Hans,

Safe to you, or to your television? For both questions, the age of your TV comes into play. If you have an older TV, especially a larger one, you're in for trouble.

All televisions use an electronic gun to shoot beams of energy at the screen, which makes the screen light up to form the picture. The bigger the screen, the more powerful the beam has to be to light up the larger area.

The older color TVs used beams with up to 25,000 volts. My monochrome monitor only uses about 2,000 volts. So what's this got to do with safety, as long as you don't stick your hand inside the cabinet?

Well, when a 25,000-volt beam slams into the screen, it's so powerful that it gives off X-rays!

So, you've been watching this boob tube for 10 years, and you haven't had a problem.

Well, you usually sit across the room in your easy chair to watch Monday Night Football, except this year, when you've decided to play with your computer. The X-rays petered out a few feet from the screen, so it wasn't a problem. Now you're pounding the keyboard with your face stuck 2 feet from the screen. Watch out!

If you leave the computer hooked up to that old 25-inch

color TV and use X-ray-proof sunglasses, then what? Well, if you have a nice bright computer image on the screen, then fall asleep, you will end up with a shadow of that image, even after you turn off the set. That powerful beam could easily burn up a portion of the screen. Viewing normal television doesn't cause the image to burn into the screen because the image is always changing. What's a person to do? Turn down the room lights or close the blinds so you can turn the brightness on the TV down a bit. Many sets do this automatically when the room light goes

Digital Dave's Tip

So, you're trying to work in the 132 column by 44 row mode on your super-duper VGA, but all those little dinky characters seem to run together, and the whole thing looks fuzzier than you remember it in the store.

I'll bet you have the brightness (that's the knob with the little sun on it) cranked. Turn it down and watch the display sharpen up. In the 80 by 24 mode, the extra fuzz fills in the gaps in the letters and smooths out the curves. In the zillion character by dinky mode, back off.

The electron beam that draws the characters on the screen is brightest in the center of the beam and tapers off at the edges. If the brightness is cranked up, the dots on the screen grow and run together. Back it off and the dots get smaller, and the display sharper.

The contrast knob gets in the act too. Vary the contrast at several different brightness levels to get an idea of how the two controls interact. I like white letters on a blue background for most text editing. I crank the contrast up and back off on the brightness for this color combo.

Using black letters on a white background is good for the fancy fonts of those super-duper word processor programs. Again, back down on the brightness to make the white appear like a piece of paper. I don't use paper that glows.

Even the black and white monitor of the Macintosh computer can benefit from a judicious adjustment of the controls.

down. Back away from the set as far as is comfortable. This is about as much protection as you can get.

Digital Dave

On the other hand, there are types of radiation that don't seem to cause any harm. There has been some warning about low-frequency magnetic waves causing problems, though I haven't seen any scientific evidence supporting these warnings. That doesn't mean there is no hazard, but I don't see where you can get away from it. If you weren't glued to the computer screen, you'd be propped up in front of the boob tube receiving those same magnetic waves.

Dear Digital Dave,

I was sitting at my computer recently typing away, and the telephone rang. I answered and noticed that there was a buzz in the ear piece. The closer I placed the receiver to the monitor (a Commodore 1902A), the louder the noise got.

It even made noise when the base of the phone was completely disconnected from the handset. What is this noise? Am I being slowly cooked by invisible radiation emanating from my seemingly peaceful monitor? Is this going to hurt me later in life?

William Eastman

Dear Will,

No, your monitor is not blasting you with harmful radiation, unless it's broken. Even if it were, you couldn't see it or hear it, with or without the aid of your telephone.

The magnetic field that steers the beam back and forth on the face of your monitor is also steering the diaphragm in your ear piece back and forth, which makes a buzzing noise.

Does this harm you? Well, the ear piece generates a magnetic field, which moves the diaphragm in time with your girlfriend's voice, and you stick that magnetic field in your ear all the time!

Digital Dave

Those monitors live on magnetic waves. Make sure they get their minimum daily allowance.

Monitor Troubleshooting

What if your monitor is not behaving like you expected? Sometimes we just don't know *what* to expect.

Dear Digital Dave,

I brought home straight "A"s on my report card, so my parents just bought me an NEC MultiSync 3D monitor and a VGA card for my computer, which I really love. It works just great and the colors are dynamite!

The problem is that the monitor sometimes makes clicking noises when I start up programs, then the screen jerks around for a bit. Does it have a problem? It's brand new, and I don't want to hurt my parents' feelings by calling it a piece of junk.

Danny Bergman

Dear Danny,

Your whiz-bang monitor is doing just what it's supposed to do. When you start up programs that use a different VGA mode, the monitor is automatically readjusting its scan rate.

There are relays, which are magnetically controlled switches, to change the monitor settings. The relays click when activated by the microprocessor inside the monitor. It takes a second or so for the synchronization circuits to catch up to the new scan rate, and for the screen to settle down.

There is nothing wrong with your monitor. Welcome to the world of high-tech video displays. I've got that same model monitor, and I think it's the greatest too!

Digital Dave

It's amazing how much the IBM PC has been upgraded over the years by swapping out components. Every once in a while though, the upgrade doesn't come off perfectly.

Dear Digital Dave,

I just bought a EGA card that I'm running with my NEC MultiSync on an IBM-XT. When I start it up, it gives me one long beep then three short beeps, yet it still completes the bootup. I'm wondering what this error is or if it is an error.

I've also been able to try the same components on an ARC XT Turbo board, and I get a "SYSTEM ERROR #4," which I can't figure out either. I have been setting the motherboard for 80-column color graphics; what else can I do?

Ralph Cumberland

Digital Dave's Tip

Turn off that color monitor at night! It needs to be turned off and on once in a while to demagnetize the screen. If you leave the display on all the time, the degaussing coil never gets a jolt of juice to erase the magnetic field that builds up, and steers the electrons that light up the little red, green and blue dots to the wrong destination.

When the picture tube is lined up, or converged, the red electron guns fire only at the red dots on the screen, and the same for the green and blue electron guns and dots. As the magnetic field builds up on the metal parts inside the tube, the electrons from one gun sneak over to light up the dots next to the one they are supposed to be lighting.

A coil of wire is wrapped around the tube to remove the magnetic field by a pulse of current when the display is turned on. If you never turn it off, then you never turn it on, and never get cleaned up.

Dear Ralph,

It's your poor old BIOS (Basic Input Output System) ROM doing its best to check out your hardware, and let you know if it got rusty overnight. In this case, it just doesn't know what to make of this newfangled EGA you plugged into it.

Since the BIOS code, which doesn't understand EGA, runs only at bootup, and the Disk Operating System (DOS) takes over and *does* handle the EGA properly, I would just call the beeps music to my ears.

Digital Dave

Here is a go-around about a monitor problem for a Commodore computer, though the fixes might work on just about any computer monitor, or even a television set.

Dear Digital Dave,

I have a Commodore 64 and I am using a 1702 monitor. My problem is the waving I get in my screen. I read an article that suggested moving the power supply away from the monitor. Well, my power supply is well away from my monitor and still I get waving. What to do?

Harry Williams

Dear Harry,

The waving could come from two sources: either the magnetic field from a power supply or motor is interfering, or the power that is being supplied to your monitor's circuits is not well filtered. Move the monitor away from all other electrical equipment, even if only for a minute for a test. If this solves the problem, rearrange your computer desk.

If it doesn't solve the problem, take your monitor in for service. It probably needs a new filter capacitor in the power supply. Monitors work with very high voltages, so get a qualified repair person to work on it.

Digital Dave

This time I had to call in the reinforcements.

Dear Digital Dave,
   Another possible solution to the fellow computerist with the wavy Commodore 1702 monitor: adjust the horizontal control. I had the same problem, and adjusting this control fixed mine. By horizontal control, I mean the control behind the pull-down panel on the front of the monitor. Hope this helps.
                                                   Tim Boucos

Dear Digital Dave,
   The question asked of you about screen interference brought to mind a problem I had. You might wish to mention to your readers that anything else on that circuit (especially that outlet) will cause problems.
   I had a fan connected to the same outlet where I have my setup, and it caused a pronounced 60-cycle roll on my screen. Thought I would mention it.
                                               Dave Nadelman

Dear Tim and Dave,
   Thanks for these tips. They are sure a lot easier to try than the things I suggested.
                                                 Digital Dave

Summary

I hope you are seeing things more clearly now. Your video display system, made up of monitor, adapter card and software, is the most obvious image to people who check out your new computer. Outfitted with the latest low-cost, high-resolution color systems, your computer can be a lot of fun, even if you are writing a term paper for school.

CHAPTER 6

Printers

What good is that report you wrote if it just sits there on your computer screen? The best word processor is worthless without being able to get your words on paper the way you want them. A printer is probably the first addition most people make to a basic computer system. And trading up to better and faster printers happens more often than trading up to new computers. I have three printers sitting here in my study, and high on my list of new goodies is a new laser printer.

Let's explore the different types of printers available for the beginner. Sure, there are 1200 dot-per-inch laser printers and color film recorders, but they can cost as much as your house and are used in the graphic arts industry. We'll stick to the printers in which the small business person or home computerist would be interested.

The most popular type of printer available is known as the dot matrix printer, though almost everything on the market these days forms the characters out of tiny dots. A better name would be a dot matrix *impact* printer, because it uses a series of tiny hammers that pound on a piece of hardened wire, poking an inked ribbon against the paper. By timing the pounding of the hammers, then sweeping the print head across the paper, characters or graphic images can be formed.

The low end of the dot matrix printer market is made up of 9-pin printers, some very cheap and slow, and some very fast, but more expensive. There are nine hammers, so each character is made up of a maximum of nine dots stacked vertically.

The upper end of the dot matrix printer market is made up of the 24-pin printers, which use 24 pins. Since the characters are made up of up to 24 dots vertically, the print quality is much better than the nine-pin printer. Beware though! There are some poorly designed 24-pin printers whose printouts actually look worse than some of the good 9-pin printers.

Other printer technologies available for under a kilobuck are thermal, ink jet, and an increasing number of laser printers. Thermal printers are very small, so they are good for taking along with your portable computer, but they require a special paper, which is very expensive.

Ink jet printers squirt the ink onto the paper, instead of using a mechanical device to hit a ribbon to transfer the ink. This works real well when everything is just right, but there have been problems with the jets getting plugged up and such. Also, most ink jet ink smears when it gets damp—not good for printing out a customer list to use on your paper route, especially when it rains.

Laser printers use a mechanism like the ones the low-end photocopiers use. But instead of grabbing an image from another piece of paper, the image is painted onto a drum with a laser. The drum is charged with electricity, which picks up a black dust, called toner, where the surface is charged. The drum rotates against the paper and the toner sticks to the paper. A heater fuses the toner to the paper so it won't smear. Why go through all this when pounding a simple piece of wire on a ribbon will make nice round dots on paper for a lot less money? The laser printer is capable of making much smaller dots, which results in cleaner-looking output.

Dot Matrix Printers

Let's look at some of the features that make one dot matrix printer different or more expensive than another. One term that's been overused by the printer companies is letter quality (LQ) or near-letter quality (NLQ).

The standard for what a business letter should look like used to be what an IBM Selectric typewriter could do. Fully formed character printers, such as a daisy wheel, were basically high-speed typewriters. Unfortunately, their high speed was pretty slow compared with even the low-end dot matrix printers, and they have disappeared from the market.

Daisy wheel printers did do LQ though, no argument. NLQ is whatever the printer sales guy could get away with. A good 24-pin printer with a new ribbon can do almost LQ, if you don't get out a magnifying glass. The NLQ from the top-end 9-pin printers is not bad, considering there are only nine dots in each column.

Dear Digital Dave,

What's the difference between an NLQ dot matrix printer that costs $500 and one that costs $200? Why does one cost more if they both do the same thing?

Dr. Alice Smathers

Dear Doc,

The $500-class near-letter quality (NLQ) printers use 18-, 21- or 24-pin heads. I have an NEC P6, which has 24 pins. As it makes a pass across the paper, it forms the character with tiny dots.

These dots are printed by pounding the pins (which are arranged in a vertical line) on the ribbon. As the line of pins

Digital Dave's Tip

Sure it's okay to be cheap with the printer paper you use for everyday program listings and such, but for that term paper or report that you used to justify buying your new, near-letter quality printer, get some decent paper.

Laser-perf or clean-perf type paper won't leave you with ragged edges. A better quality paper will be heavier, more even and accept ink better. While you're at it, get a new ribbon. You can always go back to the cheap paper and old ribbon when you're done.

is moved across the paper, some of the pins are fired, leaving the image. One pass across the paper and you're done.

The cheap printers have only nine pins, which usually results in the coarse computer printout quality we are all familiar with on the late notices on our bills. To get NLQ, the head is swept across the paper twice, resulting in the equivalent of an 18-pin head.

So what? Well, the high-priced machines are usually about three to 10 times as fast in the NLQ mode, and a lot quieter. Also they tend to be better built, and last longer pounding out all those late notices in the office.

Digital Dave

Since the 24-pin printers use more pins, and much smaller pins, I hear from readers with concerns about their reliability as compared to the standard 9-pin printers.

Dear Digital Dave,
I like the print quality of the 24-pin printers, and the price has come down, but I've heard that they're not as reliable as the 9-pin printers. Are the 24-pin printers a bad buy?
Jamie Summers

Dear Jamie,

I've read that too, but I don't believe it. My NEC P6 is a few years old now, and I crank a lot of paper through it, especially new copies of programs I'm writing. I tend to print a new one every few hours to keep track of what I'm trying to do.

I haven't had any trouble with it, whereas my old 9-pin printer died after only a few boxes of paper. Actually, it didn't die. It just quit printing the dangling part on "y"s and "g"s and such. The bottom pin on the print head wore out. Then the ribbon kept catching on the paper when it advanced.

I haven't had any of these troubles with my NEC, and

it has eaten much more paper. I think the brand of printer has more to do with its reliability than the particular print technology.

Digital Dave

My best advice for picking out a printer is to go to a store where you can actually try out various printer models. Have some similar things printed on each one you're interested in. The test pattern from one printer might not look as snappy as a special demonstration file that another has. Printing a straight text file to evaluate the character quality is easy, and is the biggest discriminating factor for most of us. Printing graphics takes a bit more time and cooperation from your salesperson, since you have to install a printer driver for each different printer model. If you intend to print a lot of graphics, and have narrowed the field down to two or three printers, printing a comparison image would be a worthwhile exercise.

While you're in the store buying the printer, you might as well pick up the other goodies that it takes to feed a hungry printer. You need some paper, and though a ribbon comes with the printer, a spare is in order. Is the tractor feed (the roller thing that pushes or pulls the paper through the printer) an option, or does it come in the box? Finally, we need something with which to hook the printer up to the computer, and something to prop the printer up so you can get the paper under it out of the way.

Making Connections

Speaking of hooking up the printer to your computer, which one of those holes do you plug it into? Computers have connectors on the back for many different widgets, such as a mouse, joystick, modem or your printer. These connectors, and the electronics inside the computer that make them work, are called ports. Almost every computer comes with at least one printer port, though they come in two different flavors.

Dear Digital Dave,

I was talking to my neighbor the other day, telling him that we have a LaserJet printer and a dot matrix printer at work. I told him we were using the COM port for the laser and LPT for the dot matrix. He told me this was backwards.

Could you explain the difference between COM and LPT ports, and serial and parallel printers?

Ira Goldstein

Dear Ira,

In a way, your neighbor is right. A laser printer can usually eat more data more quickly than a serial printer, so it should have the faster parallel port, but that's not how it is in the real world. The COM (COMmunications) port is a computer connection where the bits come out in a serial stream, one at a time, eight in a row to make up one character, plus a few more bits to denote the beginning and end of the character. The parallel interface used by the LPT (LinePrinTer) port sends out all eight bits at once on eight separate wires.

It's hard to find a dot matrix printer with a serial interface, so you're stuck with hooking it up to LPT1 or LPT2. It is customary for laser printers to have a serial interface, for some reason I can't figure out, so plugging it into COM1 or COM2 is where it's at. It works, and it's the way everybody does it, so don't rock the boat!

Digital Dave

Digital Dave's Tip

Try one of those new printer stands that holds your printer on an angle. You can't get a whole box of paper under them, but they take up a lot less space than a floor-type printer stand. I just gave away my old printer stand and put my printer on top of a file cabinet. Besides, when was the last time you printed anything that took a whole box of paper?

In an IBM PC or clone, the LPT and COM ports are located on plug-in cards that you buy separately. PC-DOS has provisions for two LPT ports, LPT1 and LPT2, and two COM ports, numbered the same way. You can manage more than two of each, but let's not get in over our heads here.

Since these ports are on plug-in cards, they usually provide a way for you to designate them LPT1 or LPT2. You make this selection with little jumpers or tiny switches before you even plug the card into the computer chassis. It's a real good idea to label the port number on the outside of the computer near the connector. I'm always plugging a printer into one port or another, then having to change it because I forgot which port was which.

Most cards come set up from the factory as LPT1. What if you forget to make the selection for the second card you install in your computer?

Dear Digital Dave,
    I have two LPT1s. Why? How come nothing will print?
                            Harry Finkster

Dear Harry,

Your computer is confused, that's why. How would you talk if you had two mouths?

Your machine has special addresses for the Input and Output (I/O) ports, just like memory addresses in RAM. If there are two pieces of hardware plugged into the same I/O address, the computer doesn't know which one to listen to.

Even though the printer port (LPT1 is short for Line PRinter #1) is mostly output, there are some busy signals that come back from the printer that go to input pins. This is probably what's upsetting your computer.

The solution is to re-program one LPT1 to be an LPT2. Standard practice is to have the printer port on the display adapter be LPT1, and the other port, on whatever card, be LPT2.

Usually some tiny switches or plug blocks on the I/O card need to be changed. Consult the instruction manual, or get someone to lend a hand. It's not hard to do.

Digital Dave

Ready to Print?

Let's get on to using your printer to print something. How about something easy, to start with. Printing straight text files is easiest, because most printers can do it without special commands. (Those special commands are the biggest source of headaches, but let's save that until later.)

Most programs come with text files on the disk. Public domain and shareware usually have the whole manual on the disk as a FILENAME.DOC. Most commercial programs have at least one READ.ME file to include changes that came too late to be printed in the book. After backing up your original disks, the next thing you should do is print out those .DOC files and read them.

Dear Digital Dave,

I'm relatively new to the world of MS-DOS syntax. I need help in directing the contents of a .DOC file to the printer, since many programs have these very valuable "DOCs."

I've tried just about every syntax combination I can think of. Can you help?

Mike Parker

Dear Mike,

The exact syntax depends on how your printer is hooked up to your computer, but the basic idea is that you're going to copy a file from one device to another. Now a device, to DOS, can be a disk drive, a keyboard, a monitor or even the printer.

Usually you have your printer hooked up to the primary printer port, and you would type COPY FILE.DOC LPT1 (where FILE.DOC is replaced with the name of the file) to copy the document file to the printer. If the printer is plugged into the secondary printer port, then replace the LPT1 with LPT2. You see, it does make some sense.

It gets more complicated if you're using a serial printer. You have to use the MODE command twice before you can use COPY. The first time is to set up the serial port baud rate and the rest of those parameters. I figure you already know this part, if your printer works. The second time is to redirect the printer output to the serial port. The syntax is: MODE LPT1=COM1.

Digital Dave

It's possible to screw up even a straight text file. Usually a bit of poking around the original file with your editor, and a close look at the errant printout, will reveal a simple problem.

Dear Digital Dave,

Sometimes I encounter strange results when I enter the command COPY *.DOC PRN from my Leading Edge computer to my Epson RX-80 printer. Some documents print out okay, but other documents have a different form-feed for each page.

These documents are manuals included on program disks. This causes the perforation to be everywhere except between each page, where it should be. All DIP switches are correctly set. Any suggestions?

Clarence Kemp

Dear Clarence,

I run into the same problem. It seems that every programmer who writes public domain software thinks everybody in the world owns the same printer and word processor program as he or she. Well, it just isn't so, as you and I have found out. I've spent whole evenings reformatting the documents that came with a new whiz-bang program, so they'd print properly.

Some software writers try to solve the problem by putting in enough line feeds to force the printer to move to a new page. If they have their printer set to six lines per inch, and you have yours set to eight lines per inch, guess what happens? Try switching the line spacing and print again.

Digital Dave

The reason printing straight text files is so easy is that all of the normal text characters are represented by a code called ASCII, which every printer on the market these days understands. Even so, there are some points of confusion.

For instance, there is a character called a carriage return that moves the print position back to the left margin. There is also a character called a line feed that moves the print position down to the next line. When the computer gets to the end of a line, it needs to return to the left and to go down one line. Normally both the carriage return and the line feed are sent and everybody is happy. The problem comes in when the printer is set to an auto line feed mode, where the printer automatically goes down one line when it receives a carriage return.

Dear Digital Dave,

Everything I print on my printer comes out double spaced! I can't stand this anymore. I went back to the computer store and they said it was a printer problem. The printer people tell me to get a new cable. Can you, in your infinite wisdom, help me?

Sam Hayden

Dear Sam,

One thing I can say for sure: Getting a new cable won't solve the problem. Chances are the computer is fixing a problem it thinks the printer has, and the printer is fixing a problem it thinks the computer has. When you fix a problem twice, double spaced lines are what you end up with.

Two characters are normally at the end of every line of printing. One is called the carriage return, which moves the print head back over to the left side of the page. The second one is called a line feed, and it makes the paper move up one line. Some computers, or some programs you might run on your computer, will only send out one character at the end of a line, usually the carriage return. Most printers are designed to make up for this by automatically adding a line feed after each carriage return. You can see what you end up with when the computer sends the line feed and the printer automatically adds another.

Drag out your printer manual and check the setup procedure, usually involving a bunch of tiny DIP switches. One of the switches should control the automatic line feed. Set it to the other position, and your problem should be solved.

Digital Dave

The real problems crop up when software tries to use non-standard characters like smiley faces, or foreign language characters that are not part of the United States version of the codes.

Dear Digital Dave,
   What exactly is the difference between printer ASCII and normal ASCII?

Edwin Kane

Dear Ed,
   First, the real name of the standard code is USASCII, for USA Standard Code for Information Interchange, but that's kind of hard to pronounce, so everybody just calls it "ask-ee." Through ASCII, your computer, which only really understands binary numbers, can deal with the text and numbers you can read.

Now, the official code only uses seven bits, which gives you 128 different characters and control codes. Both upper- and lower-case letters, numbers and punctuation are included.

Since most computers work with 8-bit bytes (256 possible combinations), there is room for 128 more characters. Many computers and printers use these extra (but undefined by ASCII) codes for graphics.

Also, many of the control codes are not used by personal computers and printers, so additional graphics characters get stuck in there. The same general idea was used to extend the ASCII character set to graphics, but since there are no standards, many different, and incompatible, printer codes are now in use.

Digital Dave

Printer Software

Now that we have the interface between the computer and printer hardware taken care of, there is the software to worry about. Yes, there is software in your printer. In fact most printers have a more powerful computer inside them than the computer on your desk. The software is in ROM, or Read-Only Memory. Since the operator interface is limited to a few buttons and lights on the front panel, you don't often think of interfacing to the printer's software. To do anything fancy, like changing fonts or printing italics, your computer software has to know a lot of things about the commands your printer software expects.

Dear Digital Dave,

I bought a new, inexpensive, no-name (well, I never heard of it before) printer through mail-order. The printer works fine, but the documentation has problems.

The book that came with the printer explains how to use it, but not very well. For instance, to go into special modes it uses something called an escape sequence, and they show

things like "^[SO" to turn the enlarged print mode on, and "^[SI" to turn it off.
I would like to access these modes in my programs, especially my word processor. What does all this mean?

Roger Fox

Dear Roger,

First, let's talk about what an escape sequence is, then we'll talk about what the escape is. Does that sound like double talk?

There are only 128 official characters that your computer can transmit to a printer. Some computers and printers (like IBM) cheat and allow 256, to supply foreign language and graphics characters, but those aren't escape sequences.

An escape sequence is a trick where a series of characters is made to act like one control character that isn't in the standard set. In the old days of Baudot teleprinters, the code for a capital "A" was the same as for a lower case "a." To send "A," a shift control character would be sent, and all characters thereafter would be capital, until an unshift character was sent.

An escape sequence is sort of the same, except there usually isn't an unescape used. After the receiver figures out what escape sequence was sent, it goes back to assuming normal characters.

The "^[" part of the escape sequence is a backwards way of saying escape character. If you hold down the control key (indicated by the "^") and press the "[" (look hard, it's right under the "{" on the right side of the keyboard), you will have typed the escape character. Follow it up with the rest of the escape sequence characters to get the action you want. In BASIC, CHR$(27) will generate the escape character for you.

The escape sequences you mention sound like Epson printer controls. Set up your word processor for an Epson FX series printer, and you should enjoy the additional features of your printer automatically.

Digital Dave

Since dealing with all those escape sequences is a pain, most computer software does it for you. The problem is that there are many different escape sequences used by different printer manufacturers. The software folk have solved this problem by using what they call a printer driver. It's a little file with a translation from the software's internal commands to those nasty escape sequences for your particular printer. The trick is to get the right printer driver installed in your software.

Dear Digital Dave,
   What is a printer driver?

Julia Johnsen

Dear Julia,
   A printer driver is a piece of a program that is written to send data and commands to a particular type of printer. Many printers have special features, and there is no standard way to command these features, so the printer driver was invented.
   Instead of trying to write the pieces of the program that support all the different printers into one large program, the different printer drivers are set up as separate files. When you install or set up a program the first time you use it, one of the things you'll do is select your printer driver from a menu. The program uses only the driver for your particular printer.
   My word processor comes with about three dozen printer drivers—so many that they have to be kept on a separate floppy disk. As part of the installation, you pick out the driver that works with your printer, and the install program automatically copies it over to the working disk.
   As new printers come on the market, software houses don't have to release new versions of their programs. They just send out copies of the new printer drivers to those who need them.

Digital Dave

You might be able to get away with a generic printer driver for writing simple letters, assuming they are in English. To get at the strange letters and marks you need for foreign languages, you need to get the printer driver installed for your specific model of printer.

Dear Digital Dave,

I'm using WordStar 2000 on an XT clone, and just bought the new Epson LQ 500 printer. How can I get this system to print the extended IBM character set?

I am especially interested in being able to print diacritical marks found in foreign languages, but haven't found a way to tell the printer to print what the screen shows, even by changing the DIP switch settings.

If the computer understands the ASCII codes and shows the appropriate character(s) on screen, does this mean that the word processor software is the culprit? Is there software available that will allow this problem to disappear without my having to buy a new word processor?

Chuck Bellamy

Dear Chuck,

The software is the culprit, all right. The printer just does what it's told. Epson is cranking out new models so fast that I can't keep up with the capabilities of them all, and the software manufacturers can't, either.

To solve this problem of keeping up with all the new printers that come on the market, the word processor writers came up with the idea of a separate printer driver for each type of printer. The proper driver is integrated with the word processor by the installation program you run when you set up the word processor the first time.

I have no idea what type of printer you have *WordStar* set up for now, but if your problem is with the special characters only, you're lucky.

Rerun the installation program and find the printer driver that's the closest to the LQ 500. It's probably the LQ 1500. Try it. In any case, write to MicroPro and ask for an update for the LQ 500 driver. They should provide it free.

Digital Dave

Printing Graphics

Enough of printing characters. How about some pictures? Sure, you've properly installed the printer driver in your paint program, but they're usually easier to take care of than word processor printer drivers.

> *Dear Digital Dave,*
> *I print a lot of graphics, like awards and licenses, on my dot matrix printer, and most of the time the lines of print get crooked, which really doesn't look good. Is there anything I can do about it? The first couple of lines are the biggest problem.*
>
> *Don Schultz*

Dear Don,

You have a registration problem, which has been the bane of every printing method known to man. In your case, the solution is easy because you're printing only in one color in a single pass.

Here are a few tricks.

First, use a tractor feed setting, not the single-sheet friction feed setting. The tractor feed has pins that go through the holes in the edge of the continuous computer paper and positively align it.

If your printer has a bottom feed, use it so that the paper has a straight through path and won't snag. A good printer stand is a must to use the bottom feed. A floor-model stand, as opposed to the desktop type, is better because the paper hangs straight down most of the time.

If the above doesn't get you good registration, try doing a form feed to move to the next sheet before printing. I know this wastes paper, but it keeps the paper better aligned (and you can always use the extra sheets as scratch paper).

Oh, one other thing. Don't tear the paper off every time you print a page. The more printing you do without touching the paper, the better the alignment will remain.

Digital Dave

Printing Tips and Tricks

If you have a printer that uses a ribbon, and you buy a program that prints a lot of graphics, either buy stock in a store that sells you ribbons, or buy a ribbon re-inker. Printing graphics wears out ribbons much faster than printing characters, especially if you're into dark backgrounds.

Just put the used-up ribbon (assuming the fabric isn't worn out) in the re-inker and crank away. Out comes a re-inked ribbon that's ready to go back in your printer. I would re-ink the ribbons right before using them so they don't dry out before you get a chance to use them.

Get some of the cheap plastic gloves to wear while changing the

---

Digital Dave's Tip

If you want a real clean copy of a graphic image from your computer, and all you have is a dot matrix printer, print it oversize, then reduce it with a photocopy machine. Use a new ribbon and clean white paper in your printer.

By building an image larger than the finished copy, the number of dots in the image is increased, and the reduction in the photocopy machine gives much finer resolution.

ribbon on your printer. The thin, clear plastic ones you get at the gas station would do fine, and you can dispose of them after each use. Getting the ink out of your fingertips if you don't use gloves only takes two or three days, but getting it off the pretty white textured plastic of your printer is impossible.

Ribbons aren't the only things that get worn out and used up easily. Toner cartridges can also be a huge expense, especially if you print a lot of graphics.

> *Dear Digital Dave,*
>
> *I have a LaserWriter for my small business. I am very happy with the printer, but the cost of new toner cartridges is killing me. I've seen ads for reloaded cartridges. They're much cheaper. Are these safe? Do they work properly?*
>
> *Morel Steiner*

Dear Morel,

The most delicate parts of the laser printer engine are contained in the toner cartridge. That's why they are replaceable. Usually the toner is used up and the rest of the parts, like the drum, are perfectly good.

The cartridge recharging people have to take in your old cartridges so they have something to recharge. The trick is to find a place that will recharge your own cartridges and return them to you. That way you can control the condition of the cartridge and how many times it gets recharged.

Digital Dave

A printer is the first and last peripheral added to any computer setup. It's the first thing you need to plug in, because you need hardcopy to show off your work, and it's the last because you're always upgrading to a higher resolution, faster model. Go for it!

CHAPTER 7

Modeming

People often think of computerists as nerds who stay up late in their bedrooms, withdrawing from the rest of the world by playing with their computers. Little do they know that many times, computerists stay up late to take advantage of lower telephone rates and telecommunicate with others around the globe.

Yes, computers are good not only for calculating spreadsheets or the trajectory of missiles in *F-15 Strike Eagle*. You can use them to interact with others far away who share your interests. Those interests are not confined to hacking, computer-oriented stuff. There are groups swapping stamps, coins, heritages and even making dates and getting married. And, of course, all sorts of games, from chess to airplane flight simulators complete with aerial dog fights, are flying back and forth across the wires.

> **Dear Digital Dave,**
> **Is there any way that I can play chess with my friend over the phone line with a computer and a modem?**
>
> **An Lam**

Dear An,

My first inclination was to tell you to sign up for the CompuServe on-line information service and play chess with whomever you want over the telephone line. They have a ton of games to share, but unfortunately, chess is not on my copy of their list of available games.

Since you didn't tell me what type of computer you have, I don't know where to look for an on-line version of chess. There are several versions of chess available in public domain libraries for different computers. Most have the source code available, so you could modify a chess program to use the modem interface for one of the players.

I guess the simplest way you could accomplish "modem chess" would be to use a modem program, like a recent version of *Procomm*, that allows you to call another computer and leave messages for another player. You could send the standard notation for chess moves, and each of you would maintain your own chessboard.

Digital Dave

As I said, people are doing almost everything computer-to-computer. CompuServe even likes to advertise how many couples have met, romanced, and finally gotten together face-to-face to get married!

Bulletin Board Systems

For new users, it's a mystery that electronic Bulletin Board Systems (BBSs) are not owned by large corporations. The magic of it all is that it costs very little to set up a BBS, and yet it's such a powerful communications tool.

Dear Digital Dave,
Why are Bulletin Board Systems (BBSs) free? What kind of phone systems are used?

Dan Webb

Dear Dan,
Not all BBSs are free. Commercial ones, like Compu-Serve, charge a fee for the time you spend on-line. Even some of the amateur BBSs are asking for a sign-up charge.

Most of the local BBSs are personal computers, ranging from Radio Shack Color Computers to IBM's latest top-of-the-line machine. People get a thrill out of building a system from the many pieces of available hardware and software.

Many boards are nothing more than an Apple II, with a couple of floppy disk drives and a modem plugged into the ordinary phone line in a kid's bedroom.

Seems like magic!

Digital Dave

Here's a few letters about the ins and outs of using BBSs. Using a BBS is actually pretty simple if you just read what's on the screen and make your choices from what you see.

Often when you call a BBS and ask to look at a long text file, it scrolls off the top of the screen too quickly (especially at 2400 baud). On most BBSs, you can stop the text by pressing "P" for pause. On others, try holding down the control key and pressing the "Q." Control-S usually starts the text again.

Dear Digital Dave,
When using a BBS, after pressing "P" to pause the text scroll, how do you get the text moving again?
Art Shepheard

Dear Art,
On a BBS that uses a "P" to Pause, use an "S" to Start. They couldn't use "S" to Stop for obvious reasons.
On other systems try Control-S to stop (hold down the control key and press "S"), and Control-Q to start. Don't ask what "Q" stands for.
Digital Dave

My only guess is that the Q key is easy to reach when your pinky finger is on the control key.
Here are a few other things to learn when you get started with BBSs. First, the BBS needs to know the screen characteristics of your computer so it can send text in a readable form.

Dear Digital Dave,
I just purchased a modem (US Robotics Direct 1200PC) and dialed a local BBS. Please explain what is meant by "terminal width," "line feeds," and "how many nulls?" The BBS asked these questions when I first came on-line. Thanks.
Roger Lee

Dear Roger,
The BBS was just trying to get to know you a little better. Since that was the first time you logged onto that particular

bulletin board system, it wanted to know how big your screen was and what kind of control characters to send so your screen wouldn't get garbled up.

The terminal width is the number of characters your screen can display on one line. Most computers display 80 character lines, so the terminal width would be 80. Some older home computers can only fit 32 or 40 characters on the screen, especially if you're using a television for a screen.

If you have line feeds set incorrectly, you'll know it quickly. The incoming text will run over itself, all on the same line, and you won't be able to read a word. That means you need the BBS computer to send you a line feed. A line feed merely "feeds" a new "line" to the receiving computer, so the text won't run over itself.

It your text is showing up double spaced, that means both computers are adding line feeds. So answer "no," because you don't need a second line feed.

Nulls are dummy characters that get stuck at the end of lines to give your output device (your screen) time to get the cursor back to the left side before printing more characters. Unless you're using a printer instead of a screen, you usually don't need nulls, so answer "0." If you miss characters at the beginning of lines, increase the number of nulls until the problem goes away.

Now this sounds like a real hassle, and you don't want to go through this every time you log on. Well, computers are built to be user friendly, and as long as you log onto that BBS with the exact same name, it will remember all this stuff and take care of it for you.

Digital Dave

I know that all sounds rather vague, but once you log onto a BBS and get it set up right, it will become obvious. Most BBSs remember all this stuff the first time you log on and establish a user name. That's why it asks you where you're calling from, so it can tell the difference between Joe Shmo from Poodunk, KY and Joe Shmo from Farout, MO.

Commercial BBSs

Not all BBSs are toys in somebody's bedroom. The biggest BBSs aren't even called BBSs, but that's what they are. They prefer names like on-line telecommunications service or teletext service. All that really means is that they charge money for the use of the system—but you *do* get something more by paying for it.

The bigger services have tremendous databases available, many of which are updated frequently. Some examples include hourly news headlines, daily weather reports and stock market quotes that appear only seconds later than they appear on the big board.

CompuServe has become the standard by which all the other commercial BBSs are judged, because it is the biggest. On the other hand, by being the biggest, it has to cater to all users, regardless of what type of computer they own.

There is a relatively new kid on the block, Prodigy, which uses its own telecommunications software. The software works only on an IBM or Macintosh computer. What does the software do? It adds graphics, that's what. CompuServe may have a few pictures that you can download and display, but Prodigy does everything in a graphics mode.

> *Dear Digital Dave,*
> *What do you think of the new on-line system, Prodigy, as opposed to the old standby CompuServe?*
> *Stanley Stevens*

Dear Stan,
I sent away for Prodigy's free start-up kit. I figured I couldn't lose. While I've only tried Prodigy out a few times, I've been using CompuServe for years.

CompuServe has no minimum monthly fee, but the bill adds up quickly if you use it a lot. Prodigy has a 12 dollar flat monthly fee, with some extras for special services. CompuServe is a simple, text-based service available to any computer. Prodigy is machine-specific because the displays are graphics oriented. At this point, it works only with a PC or clone, or a Macintosh.

CompuServe has come to the rescue for my daughter a few times when she got behind on her school work, and we've used the on-line encyclopedia to look up information for a paper. Prodigy, too, contains an on-line encyclopedia.

The biggest difference between the two services is speed. Don't even dream of using Prodigy at less than 2400 baud. That flashy graphics interface really slows down the response time. With a text-based on-line system, you can at least read the text as it crawls across your screen at slower baud rates. Prodigy just sits there flashing a "working" sign at you until the screen is downloaded.

Many of the displays are pretty hokey, but I like the weather map. As more features become available, and they have time to take advantage of the graphics capabilities, I think Prodigy will be a lot of fun.

Digital Dave

Buying a Modem

Let's examine what to look for when buying a modem. Modems come in different speeds, like 300, 1200, 2400 and 9600 baud. Modems can be internal or external. Which is best for you?

Dear Digital Dave,
I am looking to buy a modem. Some say they are Hayes compatible, while others say they use the AT command set. Which is better?

Gordy Arwood

Dear Gordy,

If a modem uses the AT command set, it's already Hayes compatible; the two terms mean the same thing. Just about all of the modems designed in the last several years are AT command set/Hayes compatible. This is just a series of short words and letters your modem program uses to set the operating parameters of the modem.

Most good modem programs can be customized to operate with non-standard modem command sets, but that's a hassle, so the modem makers have settled on using the same commands as Hayes.

Digital Dave

As with everything else having to do with a computer, modeming can be a bit more complicated than buying a toaster and plugging it in. Sometimes you need a few more pieces to make it work. Then you have to spend a bit of time learning how to use it.

Dear Digital Dave,

I have a TRS-80 Model III, and need to communicate with my school's computer over the phone lines. My professor told me all I need is a modem, and that they cost about $70 each. Do I need anything else?

Matthew Wiley

Dear Matt,

First, let's make sure that we have the hardware squared away. The stock Model III doesn't come with a place to plug in the modem, so you need a serial or asynchronous port. It's a plug-in card that has a 25-pin connector on it.

The modem has to be a "stand-alone" model. The internal modems meant for an IBM PC or Apple II will not work. You want one that comes in its own separate box with its own power supply.

For $70, you're probably going to get a 1200 baud modem.

For about another $50, you should be able to get a 2400 baud model, which goes twice as fast. It's your time and money, so decide which is more valuable. If you plan to do many long-distance modem hookups, then the 2400 baud modem will pay for itself very quickly.

Next, we need to take care of the software. Just plugging in a modem doesn't allow your computer to talk to the world. You need a program that tells your computer how to use the modem.

There are quite a number of modem programs in the public domain, especially if you're running the CP/M operating system on your Model III. *MODEM7* is a popular one.

There are a few things to think about when selecting a modem program. Do you want to emulate a particular type of computer terminal? For example, if the computer at school is a VAX, then you'd want a modem program that can emulate a VT-100 terminal. IBM mainframes need IBM terminals, and so on.

The modem program should also support file transfers of the type available on your school's computer. *KERMIT* is a popular file transfer protocol on institutional computers. It's in the public domain, and the version of *KERMIT* that runs on your Model III would be a good starting point for a modem program.

Digital Dave

As I mentioned, modems use different speeds, and the modems on both ends of the telephone line need to use the same speed. This is not as bad as it seems at first, because every modem I know of runs at its rated speed, and if that doesn't work, it tries the lower speeds.

For instance, if you have a 1200 baud modem, and you call up a BBS with a 2400 baud modem, the modems will squeal at each other for a few seconds, then the BBS modem will decide that its high speed isn't working, and it will automatically switch to 1200 to match your modem.

Dear Digital Dave,
    I recently purchased a used Hayes 300. I brought it home, and to my dismay the ID sticker on the bottom reads, "Smartmodem 1200." Anyway, the modem works fine at 300 baud, but if I switch to 1200, it prints out trash.
    Is there a way I could find out if my modem works only in 300 baud, or if the modem is busted or disabled?
                                                                    Greg Burton

Dear Greg,
    To your "dismay" the ID sticker reads Smartmodem 1200, and you paid for a 300? I think you got a bargain. People are dumping 300 baud modems because the 1200 baud modems have come down in price.
    When you fire up your computer and start sending commands to your modem at 300 baud, it locks up at that rate. Try turning off your modem, then reset your computer to 1200 baud, and turn on the modem and send a message. It should work fine at 1200 baud.
                                                                    Digital Dave

Modem Programs

    Almost every modem comes from the manufacturer with a copy of one modem program or another. Since most modems use the same AT command set, don't feel tied down to that particular modem program. It could be just the cheapest one the manufacturer could get his hands on, or maybe he was too cheap to include one at all.

Dear Digital Dave,
    I received a new modem for my birthday, but I don't have a modem program to run it. You suggested **Procomm,** *which is a good, inexpensive shareware program. But since I don't have a modem program, I can't download it from a BBS. How do I get a copy?*
                                                                    Jon Hendrix

Dear Jon,

The brute force method of obtaining *Procomm* is to send off a check for $25 to: Datastorm Technologies, Inc., P.O. Box 1471, Columbia, MO 65205, but that's not in the spirit of shareware and modeming.

A quicker way, and one in the spirit of things, is to go to the house of a friend with a modem program, and call up the *Procomm* distribution BBS for the latest copy. The number is: (314) 474-8477.

You can go ahead and use *Procomm*, but it will remind you of the registration fee several times. After you have paid your fee for registration, you will be given a telephone number and a password on a BBS which provides support for *Procomm*. Also, they hustle you to send in fifty more smackeroos for a copy of *Procomm Plus*. It already has too many features for my taste, but some people want it to be an end-all program. It's getting close to that.

Digital Dave

Modem Troubleshooting

Let's wrap this chapter up with some straight out modem problems. Besides figuring out how to make the modem work, the biggest problem is a noisy phone line. Since you are not listening directly to the sounds that are coming over the line, it's sometimes hard to tell what's really going on.

Dear Digital Dave,

While recently trying to communicate with CompuServe and other BBSs, I received some gibberish and missing/ added characters. What is the cause of this? Incorrect baud rate?

John Borox

Dear John,

If the baud rate were wrong, all of the data would be gibberish. The problem is noise on the telephone line. This noise could be the telephone company's problem, or it could be somebody in your own house picking up an extension phone.

I've had this problem with my kids, so I rewired my phone lines and put in a switch that cuts off all the extension phones when I go on-line with my modem. It's also useful to cut short teenagers when they hang on the phone for hours.

Digital Dave

Dear Digital Dave,

I have a 110/300/1200 modem. I have never run 110 baud, but I have run 300 baud successfully. When I run 1200 baud however, things run OK for a while and then I get random characters on the screen, the screen flashes colors, and the BBS I'm in contact with also appears to receive these characters.

When this occurs, the "receive" data light flashes but not the "send" data light. What is the most likely problem?

Bob Ellis

Dear Bob

When the "receive" data light flashes, it means the modem thinks it is receiving data. Well, in this case it received some noise that looked like data to the modem, so it sent the mistaken data to the computer screen. When the modem is in the 300 baud mode, it mistakes noise for data more easily than in the 1200 baud mode.

Now, what is the cause of this noise? Usually somebody else in the house picked up an extension phone, then hung it up when they got a burst of noise instead of a dial tone. The next most likely cause would be a noisy telephone line. There isn't much you can do, other than hanging up and calling again. You might want to wiggle your telephone cable a bit and see if it causes the problem. A lose connection is rare for a phone cable, but it's the only problem that can be fixed easily.

Digital Dave

Not all problems are caused by noise on the phone line, of course. Getting the computer to communicate with the modem is the first step, and every combination of computer and modem has its idiosyncrasies. Here's a writer who helped me out for a change.

Dear Digital Dave,

I don't know if anyone else has had problems getting their Apple IIgs to work through its original modem port or not. I did, and was told by both the local computer store and the Apple rep that I needed a Super Serial Card to make most modem programs work.

The April issue of A+ *magazine carried the answer in a very well written article on Apple communications. The default value on the "Control Panel" modem settings are wrong. You need to set the DCD and the DSR/DTR handshake to the "No" position.*

You also have to ensure that the slot 2 setting is "modem port." I now use the MouseTalk *program with good results. By the way, the computer store took back my SSC and gave me a refund.*

Gary Snyder

Dear Gary,

Well, I finally get a letter from somebody with a new computer and a solution to a problem! Thanks for the great advice!

Digital Dave

Summary

We only scratched the surface of the many ways to use your computer to reach out and touch someone. There are uses for almost everybody. Lawyers and doctors tap into computer databases of case studies instead of thumbing through huge volumes in the library. Speaking of libraries, they are moving away from print media and making use of computer telecommunication to give users wider access to their materials. I know the librarian at work spends more time on the computer terminal than fingering the card file. The cost of modems has dropped drastically in the last few years, as the size and number of on-line services has exploded. Don't be shy, get out there and telecommunicate!

PART III

CHAPTER 8

Operating a Computer

This chapter is a collection of things to do, and things not to do, with your computer. Some of this advice is just plain common sense, but it doesn't occur to most people until it's too late. Let's start off with the real disasters.

> **Dear Digital Dave,**
> **Is it okay to compute during a thunderstorm?**
> **Julliet Gibson**

Dear Julliet,

No! Absolutely not.

If a thunderstorm wakes me up in the middle of the night, I jump out of bed and run to my study and yank the power cord for all my computer equipment. Don't forget to unplug the telephone line to your modem.

Those plug strips with the surge arrestors are good for stopping spikes from lightning hits to the power line five miles away, but they are pretty useless for close strikes. If you should suffer a direct hit, nothing helps.

Lightning struck a building near where I work. The VAX computers survived because they are protected by power conditioners that take a forklift to move, but the computer terminals in the building were scrapped. Some even melted, case and all. The only one that made it wasn't plugged in. That's the cheapest and best lightning protection.

On top of all this mayhem, if you actually try to process data during a thunderstorm, even lightning strikes far away can upset your computer and scramble your data. Take a rest from computing, but don't take a bath either.

Digital Dave

Please Don't Hurt the Computer

Computers can be frustrating, but stay in control!

Dear Digital Dave,
    I got mad at my computer last night, so I threw an orange at it. The juice leaked down into the monitor. Now I'm afraid to turn it on again. What should I do?

Stephen Frankenburn

Dear Steve,
    No use crying over spilled orange juice. I assume that there is no crack in your screen or any other obvious damage to the monitor. If there is, do not plug it in. Take it to a repair shop.

If the sticky mess is the only problem, make sure the monitor is unplugged from the wall and the computer. Clean up the outside of the cabinet with a damp (not wet) rag.

Do not disassemble the cabinet. There are all sorts of dangerous things, both electrical and mechanical, inside that monitor. Let the technician in the shop break the neck off the picture tube if anything needs to be done on the inside. Then he gets to pay for a new picture tube if he has an accident.

If only a little juice dribbled into the cabinet, let the whole thing dry out for a couple of days, then plug it in and give it a try. You're running the risk of letting the juice corrode some of the parts inside by leaving it there, but the cost of getting it cleaned out might exceed what the monitor is worth.

Digital Dave

SR

Digital Dave's Tip

Your computer must breathe. It doesn't generate much heat, except in very small spots inside. To distribute the heat and move it out of the box, there is usually a fan in the power supply.

With this fan drawing air through your computer's innards, what do you think gets stuck in there? Right, dust! Take the cover off once in a while and clean it out. Make sure you unplug it first, though.

I use a soft paint brush that's never been used for painting. A little bit of blowing helps too, but I usually end up coughing.

Don't forget to dust off the monitor and clean that screen, too. It's amazing how much grime you've been looking through.

Can Your Computer Hurt Itself?

Sometimes people fear their computer is self-destructing before their very eyes.

Dear Digital Dave,
I have a Macintosh computer with an external hard drive, and I just bought a new computer desk.
The Macintosh fits into the computer desk best with the drive on the left side. My friend, who also owns a Macintosh, says I shouldn't put it there. Will having the drive on the left hurt it?

Steve Jonavitz

Dear Steve,
Putting the external drive for a Macintosh on the left won't hurt the drive, but the magnetic field from the computer's power supply, which is located on the left side, may interfere with the ability of the drive to read data correctly. If you have to be English and drive on the left side, keep it several inches away from the computer.

Digital Dave

Dear Digital Dave,
I have my disks in a Flip'N'File above my disk drive. My disk drive is about one inch away from the left-hand side of my monitor.
Will my disk be damaged from either the disk drive or the monitor? Could the disk drive itself be damaged by the monitor, or vice versa?

Michael Amster

Dear Mike,
Yes, yes, no, no.
The monitor and the disk drive cannot be damaged by magnetic fields, though their operation may be interrupted.

The floppy disks, on the other hand, are very sensitive to damage from magnetic fields.

The data is stored on the disks as tiny changes in the magnetic fields in the iron particles on the surface of the disk. Even a weak magnetic field will disturb the stored data. Keep your disks away from magnets (like the ones in your monitor), and electric motors (like the ones in your drives).

When I first got my SuperBrain (a very old computer), the magnetic field from the floppy disk drive made the whole screen wiggle every time the disk was accessed. It didn't hurt anything, but it sure looked funny.

Digital Dave

PC Mysteries

There are a few mysteries of the IBM PC design that live on, even if we forgot why they were made that way.

Dear Digital Dave,

The instructions on a number of plug-in cards for my PC say that they can't be used in "slot eight." Since the machine has eight slots, I assume it's one of the end slots. Which one? And why is this a problem? Some manuals refer to the "short slot." Which one is this?

Jerimy Schubert

Dear Jerimy,

"Slot eight" and the "short slot" are one and the same: the one closest to the power supply in an IBM XT. It's the "short slot" because the left hand disk drives would be in the way of a long card. It's "slot eight" because the slots are numbered from left to right, facing from the front.

Besides being too short for many cards, slot eight is electrically different from the rest of the slots. It has an additional signal called the "card select." Very few cards use this signal, but it has to be taken care of if you want to use that slot.

Usually, there's a DIP switch or jumper to tell a card that
it's in slot eight, and to take care of the card select signal. If
your card doesn't have this feature, plug it into another slot.
It might take some board swapping if you have a full deck.

Digital Dave

Computer Operating Tips and Tricks

Here are some tips to help you develop good computer operating practices. It often doesn't take any additional effort to have a
smoothly operating computer, just good habits.

- About once every two months when you go to turn on
  your computer for an evening of computing, don't.
  Spend the time organizing your work area. It's amazing how many lost manuals and printouts turn up in
  one of these cleanup blitzes. My only problem is that I
  need a week of evenings to clean up my mess.

- Getting a bit squeezed for space on your hard drive?
  Take a look at that DOS subdirectory where you
  copied everything from the two disks that came with
  the computer.

  If you have a true-blue PC and received both BASIC
  and BASICA, nuke BASIC, because BASICA does
  everything BASIC does, only better. Unless you're
  going to use a foreign language on your PC, dump
  KEYBIT.COM and KEYBFR.COM. or KEYB.COM.
  Then delete files ending in "BAS"; you don't need
  those dumb demo programs, and you can always recall
  them from a floppy to amuse the kids. VDISK.LST is
  only for hard-core programmers, and they can be
  grabbed from the floppy, too.

  This same philosophy also works for other programs.
  Does your word processor really need a copy of
  INSTALL.BAT on your hard drive? What about all

those printer drivers that you don't use? Clean them
out. You can always resort to the floppy library.

■ Keep a box of facial tissue near your computer. It's
good for wiping off the screen to get rid of the glare
from the dust. It's also good for soaking up the tears
from forgetting to back up that important file and
finding that you just accidentally deleted it.

Good habits are a necessity when you have a large hard drive. It's
just too easy to lose track of all those data and program files.

Dear Digital Dave,

*I agree completely with your tip about keeping things out
of your root directory! I see systems every day where the
user has put every file into the root, and overwrites half the
files daily. Then they don't understand why some programs
won't work.*

*There are a few programs that won't run from a sub-
directory, even with the PATH command set properly, especially dBASE, WordStar, Clipper and Quicksilver. The
way to get around this problem is to copy only the overlay
files to the root directory, leaving the rest of the files in their
own subdirectory.*

*The PATH command was designed to find DOS com-
mands from anywhere on the disk, and some software
doesn't incorporate the use of this feature when looking for
its other accompanying files.*

Don Bittman, President,
STAR Industries

Dear Don,

Thanks for the input. I never thought of putting only the
overlay files in the root directory to be able to use software
in more than one directory. On the other hand, I'm a fanatic
about keeping my root directory as clean as possible.

For instance, I use *dBASE III* at work a lot, so I made a dBASE3 subdirectory where I put all the files it takes to run the program. I then make subdirectories below the dBASE3 directory for the data files for each project in order to keep them separate.

When I run *dBASE*, I make sure I include the subdirectory name when I type in the data filename. Since I make a lot of command files, I only have to type the long filename once.

Digital Dave

Useful Utilities

There are a lot of little programs out there to make life easier. Many are available in the public domain, which means that you are free to use them, just don't sell them to anyone else. Besides, why would anyone want to buy something that's free? Anyway, these little gems are called utilities, and everyone has their favorite bunch. I keep a floppy full of my favorite utilities to install on every computer that I use at work.

Lately a bunch of utility programs have been assembled and sold as packages. They generally have a better user interface, and much better documentation. They still have to be used with care!

Dear Digital Dave,
A friend told me about the **Norton** Utilities, *and how they can un-erase files I've deleted. Putting this to the test, I*

Digital Dave's Tip

Instead of using the TYPE command on your PC or compatible, get a copy of a program called BROWSE, which is in the public domain. Now, instead of fighting with the control-S and control-Q to stop and start the listing on the screen, you can use the page-up and page-down keys to flip through the file. It's fast, and the price is right!

found a file I first worked on way back when I bought my computer two years ago. Suffice it to say, un-erasing the file did not fare well. In fact, several good files were trashed. Did I do something wrong? Are these quick un-erase programs valid?

Lane Spiegel

Dear Lane,

Un-erase programs can save you from committing suicide when you've *just* deleted the file with the company's entire financial history, but notice I said *just* deleted. These programs depend on one very important fact: Deleting a file does not erase any data at all, it just releases the file's storage area so new data can take its place.

In the disk directory, where the computer keeps track of all the files and their disk location, the entry for the deleted files is modified to show that all the data blocks are available to store new files. Until a new file is written to the disk, all the data is still there.

An un-erase program, like the *Norton Utilities*, goes in and modifies the directory entry back to being a valid file pointer again. If you've stored another file in the meantime, chances are you have a disk full of garbage on your hands.

Now if you really know how your disk is put together, you might be able to recover pieces of files that have been partially overwritten. But in general, the feature is only good when you suddenly realize that you shouldn't have pressed the return key, and you want to undo that last step of deleting a file.

Digital Dave

Troubleshooting

The first thing you are supposed to do when you get new software is to make a "backup" copy and a "work" copy, right? So what's the best way to do it?

Dear Digital Dave,
    When I'm making a copy of a whole disk on my PC,
should I use DISKCOPY or COPY *.*?

                                                    Janice Ferlington

Dear Jan,
    I depends on how lazy you are. A few other things get into
the act, so I'll explain. DISKCOPY is great for quick and dirty
copies. That means whatever is on the original disk will be
copied, including the particular DOS format.
    PC-DOS uses several different formats, and it's a tribute
to the operating system that changes in format are transparent
to the user. What does that mean when you're trying to copy
a diskette?
    If you're using an old diskette, especially public domain
stuff, then you don't want to use DISKCOPY, because you're
going to end up with an old format on the new diskette. Format
the new diskette with your latest version of FORMAT, then
use COPY *.* to transfer the files.
    When I want to copy an old disk, and I don't want the
old format, I use COPY *.* but it takes two steps. I create a
subdirectory on my hard disk called TEMP, then CHDIR
TEMP. I COPY A:*.*, which puts everything I want to copy
in the TEMP subdirectory on the hard disk.
    I put in the new formatted diskette, then type COPY *.*
A:, which copies it all to the new diskette. Then a DEL *.*,
after making sure I'm still in the TEMP subdirectory, cleans
off the hard disk.

                                                    Digital Dave

Once in a while a new version of a program screws up the works,
though usually it is more cosmetic than disastrous. There is always
a tricky way around it.

Dear Digital Dave,

A friend of mine set up my computer with an AUTO-EXEC.BAT to get things going right when I turned the system on. Recently I upgraded to DOS 3.1, and while the start-up still works okay, the screen gets messed up and the message "ECHO is OFF" gets printed several times.

Will this hurt my machine? My friend moved away, so I don't know how to fix it. Can you help me?

Jennifer Clandsy

Dear Jenny,

Not to fear, Digital Dave is here. Microsoft messed up some of the nice features of the BATch utility, like using an ECHO command with a blank message to leave a blank line on the screen.

Type "TYPE AUTOEXEC.BAT" and you will see the contents of the batch file that runs when you boot up. There are probably several lines that have nothing but the word "ECHO" on them.

Under old versions of DOS, the ECHO command all by itself just prints a blank line on your display, handy for making the screen look pretty. New versions will print a message telling you if the echo is on or off. I can't imagine what good this command is, but I guess the Microsoft people thought it would be more consistent with other commands that report their status when entered without parameters.

You can fix the problem by editing the AUTOEXEC.BAT file to insert a blank space and a non-printing character after each ECHO that doesn't have a parameter after it. EDLIN, the editor that came with DOS, can put in the non-printing character for you. Most editors can't deal with characters that you can't see.

Type "EDLIN AUTOEXEC.BAT" then an "L" (and a return) to list the file. Let's say line number 5 is a blank ECHO. Type "5" (return) to point at line 5. Type "ECHO " (notice the space), then hold the Alt key down and type "255" on the NUMERIC keypad (and finally a return). This will insert a space and the ASCII character 255 at the end of the line. Repeat for each ECHO that doesn't have something after it.

Type "EX" to exit, then reboot to see if things are fixed up. They should be. If not, watch the display closely to determine which line still has an ECHO without a parameter on it.

One more clinker that Microsoft threw into the latest version of the BATch command is the elimination of treating a line that starts with a period as a REMark. If there are any of these in your file, replace the periods with "REM." That wasn't so hard was it?

Digital Dave

You can't go on forever stacking things into your computer's memory. There are limits.

Dear Digital Dave,

Help! I keep running into the error message, "OUT OF ENVIRONMENT." What does that mean, and how do I cure it?

Philip Shapiro

Dear Phil,

That means we have used up all the clean air and water and your computer is choking, or something like that. Actually it did exactly what the error message said, it ran "OUT OF ENVIRONMENT" space.

The environment space is a piece of memory that DOS sets aside to remember things like your path. That's where I usually run into trouble. When my path command starts looking like a list of every subdirectory on my hard drive, I run out of environment space. Consolidate those utility and

DOS programs into a few subdirectories, shorten up your PATH command in your AUTOEXEC.BAT file, and you should be okay.

If this doesn't work, you may have too much junk stuck in your environment space by some of your programs. Clean out those pop-up programs that you have in the AUTO-EXEC.BAT, and use only what you need.

Digital Dave

Sometimes I'm too devious for my own good. Then some kind soul comes along and straightens me out.

Dear Digital Dave,
I've recently moved into a new house. Somehow, during the move, I lost all of the instruction pamphlets for my computer games.

I have friends who want to borrow games sometimes, but I'm skeptical of lending them without instructions. What should I do?

Francis M. Whalen

Dear Francis,

I would make up new instructions! All of them wrong, of course. I would hand these out to my friends who wanted to borrow my games, then beat the pants off them when they came over to play against me!

As long as your friends know how to handle the media (disk, tape or cartridge) that stores the games, then it should be impossible to damage them.

Digital Dave

Dear Digital Dave,
A game manufacturer will be happy to send you replacement manuals if you have a legitimate (believable) reason for needing them, and you've mailed in all your registration

cards. I had that experience with some very soggy manuals caused by a leaky roof. The manufacturer was almost jovial about replacing them. I hope this helps.

Nola Wilson

Dear Nola,

I'm glad somebody has had a good experience with getting manuals replaced. Back in the old days, when people in the computer industry were very trusting souls, it used to be standard practice to ask for, and sometimes pay a minimal fee to receive, manuals for programs before you even bought them!

That's how programmers got you to spend $400 for a piece of software: by letting you know exactly what you were getting. These days, programs are $14.95 at K-Mart, and you're supposed to make a selection based on a fancy packaging job.

If the manufacturer of your program provides software of the same quality as his service, then he will probably stay in business for a long time, assuming that the fly-by-night operators (who are too busy with jerky copy-protection schemes and lack of customer support), don't destroy the market first.

Digital Dave

Special operating conditions require special thought about what is best for your computer.

Dear Digital Dave,

I use my Apple IIe as a bulletin board, so it is left on day and night. I usually remove the system floppy disk and leave only the data disk. My friend says that I should leave the system disk in the drive all the time. Who is right?

George Stevens

Dear George,
    Assuming you have several backup copies of your system disk, you should leave one in the computer whenever you're not operating the system and the power is on. If there should be a power glitch, the computer will try to reboot and leave the disk drive running until you get around to sticking a disk back in. If you don't want a fried drive, leave the disk in.

Digital Dave

Questions about when to shut your computer off are very popular. Some people want to leave it on all the time, others turn it off as soon as they push the keyboard aside because they don't want to listen to the noise. As with everything else, there are trade-offs to be made.

Dear Digital Dave,
    I've heard it said that switching your computer on does it more harm that leaving it running continuously.
    Is that so? I know there's a fan in the power supply. Wouldn't continuous running burn things out eventually? Does it help to only turn off the monitor when not in use?
    If I have a 130 watt power supply, does that really mean it only uses up as much electricity as burning the same size light bulb for all that time?
    I have some TSRs which would be nice to have installed all the time without re-booting for one or two things, but I'm afraid of injuring the hardware and/or running up huge electric bills. What do you think?
    Thanks for your help.

James Fife

Dear Jim,
    Let's answer the "how much" question first. If you have a 130 watt power supply, then that's how much power it can put out. Nothing is perfect, in fact a good power supply is only

about 60 percent perfect, which means we have to put in about 217 watts to get 130 out.

That assumes you've loaded your computer up to the maximum. I'd guess you're drawing half that for an average computer. So that's about 160 watts for the computer, and probably another 40 watts for a monochrome monitor, or 75 watts for a color one.

Of course, the printer draws 100 watts if it's on, and don't forget that killer stereo that dims the lights when you really get cranking. I think I'm getting off the track here.

Yes, your computer takes a beating every time you turn it on, and the hard drive doesn't like being turned off and having to land the head on the disk.

In the office, I turn my computer on in the morning and off when I leave for the night. At home, I turn it on the first time I use it, and off before bed.

Digital Dave

Who'd have thought there'd be so many rules to keep from blowing up your computer! It sounds pretty scary, but don't let it be. Just use your common sense. Computers are pretty hard to hurt, if you are reasonably careful. Even a computer crash is usually a non-violent affair, except for that guy with the orange!

Hardware Tips and Tricks

Here's a few more tips that make life easier through organization on the hardware end of things.

■ I keep a shoe box in my study near the computer. It has all the spare parts that come with the accessory boards and the blank plates I take out of the computer when new boards are added. It's amazing how many spare widgets are in there. It's sure handy when I have to work on somebody's computer to have spare parts on hand.

■ When you go to get a screwdriver to work on your computer, pick up the flashlight too. I always need the light to find the screw I dropped down inside.

■ I bought one of those power directors that have a bunch of switches for separately controlling your monitor, computer and printer. I leave all the power switches on, and turn on everything from the desktop, which saves reaching under the desk where the computer rests.

Turning the monitor and computer on separately helps by spreading out the in-rush current. Both my monitor and computer really suck the juice at power-up. The lights dim for a second.

The printer is on top of a file cabinet out of reach, so the power director saves me from getting out of my chair, and cussing when the cord on my stereo headphones doesn't reach. Also, I only turn on the printer when I am actually using it, which isn't often, saving a lot of on-time for the printer, and some of the beating my SDG&E bill takes.

There are two auxiliary switches, one of which controls my other computer. It's tempting to control the stereo with the last switch, but don't do it. Computers and audio/video equipment should stay as far apart electrically as possible. If they were all plugged into the same power director, the noise filtering between the computer and the audio equipment would be lost.

■ Clear off a part of a shelf, then keep all your software and hardware manuals handy in one spot. Even if you think you remember everything about your goodies, it's best to check that switch setting or control code in the book before trashing data.

CHAPTER 9

Hardware Problems

In this chapter, we're going to hear some of the sob stories wayward computer users tell about their hardware problems. Usually questions of this sort have about 10 percent of the information I need to give a decent answer. I have a whole file drawer full of these letters.

I selected the following letters because they address general problems with hardware. Let's hope you don't have to deal with any of these problems.

Dear Digital Dave,

I hope you can answer my question. Every once in a while, for no apparent reason, my computer locks up, strange things come on the screen and it sends out random noise. Do you know what could be causing this?

Sorry, I forgot to mention what type of computer I own. I have a Commodore 64, a 1541 disk drive, and a 1702 monitor.

Michelle Mewes

Dear Michelle,

Well, let's see what we can do about your computer trials and tribulations. Having a computer lock up with funny things on the screen is known as a computer crash in the industry. It comes with the territory. If they can keep our mainframes at work from crashing more than once a week, everybody is happy.

The garbage on the screen and the funny noises are caused by the program running away and changing the screen memory and everything else that was in the way. What you end up with is scrambled brains.

Crashes are caused by one of three things: hardware, software, or a combination of hardware and software. The hardware can have a problem, like reading a bit from memory wrong, causing the program to freeze up. These can be soft errors, unrepeatable and irreparable; or hard errors, which are the result of some sort of permanent damage and require a trip to the repair shop.

The software can have a bug in it, which causes it to go off into never-never land. This can be an endless loop where the computer just gets stuck. Or in your case, the program takes a wrong branch and tries to execute instructions outside of the program area, which trashes the screen.

And there might be a mismatch between the hardware and the software because different hardware options are plugged in or different versions of software are used.

If the problem is so infrequent that you can't make any correlation with running a particular piece of software or condition (such as the computer being warmed up for an hour), then you or even a repair shop probably won't be able to find the problem.

If, on the other hand, you can make the computer crash with a particular set of events, the crash should point to one of the above problems, and point a repairman in the right direction.

Digital Dave

Computers without fans may be quiet, but they rarely can stand having upgrades added without suffering heat stroke.

> *Dear Digital Dave,*
> *I bought a used, older model Macintosh which runs hot. It gets flaky on hot summer days. It has a memory upgrade inside that I can't do without because the software I use won't run without it. What can I do?*
>
> *Jenny Quant*

Dear Jenny,
Every trick in the book has been tried to cool off Macs. With the huge after-market for fans for Apple IIs, you'd think the Apple people would have learned and put a fan in the Mac. When people start stuffing extra goodies in there, it cooks!

I've seen a scheme where a chimney on top of the cabinet is supposed to create a draft and cool off the insides. I think the only draft is in somebody's head.

First of all, make sure that nothing is blocking any of the vents. Maybe you could just get by with a small room fan directed toward the cabinet. If you insist on Macking on the scorcher summer days with no air conditioning, buy your machine its own specially-made fan. There are a number of models on the market which would do the job.

Digital Dave

Macintosh fans come in all sorts of configurations, including the latest in high technology.

> *Dear Digital Dave,*
> *I just bought a memory upgrade for my Macintosh and it came with a piezoelectric, which was just a little widget with these little plastic flaps sticking out. It looks like a piece of junk. Does it work? How?*
>
> *Dave Janisit*

Dear Dave,
    Yes, it works, as evidenced by the fact that your Mac
hasn't burned down yet. Those memory upgrades strain the
power supply and generate a lot of heat all by themselves.
    It works on the principle of piezoelectric constriction,
meaning that when you put an electric field across a piece
of piezoelectric material, it distorts the physical shape. If
you put an alternating electric signal in the fan, it wiggles
the piezoelectric material, which is hooked to the plastic flaps
in such a way as to make them move back and forth and fan
the air.

Digital Dave

Keyboards take a lot of abuse. Mine has fallen off the desk several
times in its lifetime. The cable especially takes a beating. I made the
mistake of buying a keyboard with a connector on the keyboard
itself. I'm forever plugging it back in when I pull it too far away
from the computer.

Dear Digital Dave,
    I have a Compaq computer (not Compaq Plus or any-
thing) and have recently been having problems in that the
keyboard will freeze up either spontaneously or when it's
extended too far.
    When I boot up with the keyboard out too far (on my lap
when sitting at my desk) I'll see a "301" message, then
normal initiation but no keyboard function. When on a
BBS, I'll sometimes get these characters, "{ { { ," stuck in
my text as I type, for no reason.
    Where can I go? Can you recommend a computer store
with a service shop so they can look under the hood. This
situation is making me crazy!

Bobby Newmark

Dear Bobby,
My first guess is that you have a flaky connection in your keyboard cable. When you boot up, and the computer gives you the 301 error, it means it couldn't find your keyboard.

Borrow a keyboard from a friend, and see if the problem persists. If the problem is still there, you probably need a new connector on your motherboard. If the other keyboard works fine, try replacing the connector on the end of the cable.

Your local Radio Shack should have a new connector for less than the price of gas to get there. Find an electrical engineering student that knows how to wield a soldering iron to put it on for you.

If that doesn't work, throw away the keyboard and buy a new one.

Digital Dave

Adding more memory is more than just sticking new RAM chips in, especially if your machine is maxed out to start with.

Dear Digital Dave,
I have an Apple IIe with an extended 80-column card. I would like to expand the memory but don't want to pay the cost of a RAM card. I have put 256K chips on the card, but it still only sees 64K of it.

Is there any way to use this card, or do I have to buy a RAM card? There are two other chips on the card, marked 74LS374N and DM74LS245N. Do I need to replace these also for the Apple to recognize the memory?

Justyn Worrell

Dear Justyn,
I think you're barking up the wrong tree here. The problem is that the microprocessor in your Apple IIe has only 16 address lines, each of which can only be on or off (1 or 0).

With only two possible states, it can only address 2 to the

16th power (64K) locations. The 64K of RAM you had in the machine is all it can handle without pulling some tricks. Unfortunately, your board doesn't have the tricks.

Some RAM boards for the Apple will perform bank switching. The microprocessor can address only 64K at any one time, but an additional I/O port plus some software is used to create some more address lines.

These additional address lines are used to get at the RAM above 64K. The difficulty is that the software to command the I/O port to switch RAM banks must be embedded in each of the programs that are to take advantage of the additional RAM.

There aren't many software packages around that have these tweaks, and it's almost impossible to add them later. Most people end up using the additional RAM as a RAM disk.

The problems above are the major reason for the popularity of 16- and 32-bit computers, with their larger address space, over the 8-bit machines like the Apple IIe. You either need to spring for the special RAM card that lets you band switch, or, better yet, upgrade to a bigger computer that can really use more memory.

Digital Dave

Sometimes things are just too good to be true, and you end up spending a lot more money to get what you wanted than you intended. At least the following reader had his act together enough to know when to fight and when to run. Or was it just luck?

Dear Digital Dave,

I've got a strange experience to recount to you. A couple of weeks ago, I heard that a local computer store had some HesModem1s for sale at $14.95, so I ran down and bought one.

I ran home with it and proceeded to hook it up. Much to my horror, the modem was defective and seemed to "fry" my C-64. The next day I returned to the store for a new modem and to see what they'd do for my computer.

At first they (the salesman and the manager) told me that I must have been mistaken—I must have done something wrong. At my insistence they checked out the modem, and after a half hour of trying to prove to me it couldn't be the modem, they finally admitted that it was indeed a faulty modem.

They then offered me a new modem, which I cheerfully accepted. Then I asked what they intended to do about my ailing computer. The manager told me that the store couldn't be held responsible for damage caused by something they had sold!

But here is the clincher! The manager then "generously" offered to repair my computer for $40 plus parts! I had enough wits about me to decline the offer and took the machine to another store.

Imagine my astonishment when their repair technician returned (after about 5 minutes) and billed me $1 for a bad fuse! I thanked him, paid the bill, and went home with a smile on my face.

What is your comment on all this? Can the computer store really get away with that? I'll be anxiously awaiting your response.

Efrain Rosario

Dear Efrain,

Not only can they, they did! Most equipment sold today has a disclaimer with it that places the responsibility for damage to peripheral devices on the buyer.

It doesn't make good public-relations sense for a computer store to not repair damage that their faulty equipment caused. Just count yourself lucky that the modem didn't blow out every chip in your C-64!

Digital Dave

Digital Dave's Tip

Here's a tip on what to do about a problem that shows up in almost every cheap clone computer: If the speaker in your computer rattles, especially at certain frequencies, it might not be mounted securely to the chassis. A touch of silicon cement will clear up the tone.

I hope these horror stories don't scare you away from enjoying your computer. Just repeat after me: It always happens to the other guy.

CHAPTER 10

Be Glad Someone Else Asked

We saved the best for last. In this chapter we will peruse those letters you're glad someone else wrote (mostly because you're glad you don't have a disaster like that on your hands). Or, maybe you do and you just don't want anyone else to know about it. I've even included a few "Digital Dave's Tips" that I wish someone else had written.

Sometimes I think letter writers are pulling my leg, and sometimes it's hard to tell. I don't mind. Nobody ever said computers have to be serious all the time. Let's start with some of the disasters.

Dear Digital Dave,
A friend with a Turbo TI99/4A told me if I plugged my IBM AT into a 220 volt outlet I'd accelerate its clock speed to that of a '386 machine. I did this and my monitor went blank. Why?

Michael Stirewalt

Dear Mike,
I hope this letter is a joke, because it's not very funny if you really tried this. If so, the next stop for your ill-fated AT is the trash can. I guess you could save the metal case, because all the electronic parts are crispy critters.

Even if the insides could stand it, running on a higher voltage would not speed things up a bit (couldn't resist that one). The speed of the computer is set by a crystal oscillator.

People have been known to replace the crystal with one that oscillates at a higher frequency, like replacing the 6 MHz crystal with an 8 MHz one. You can't hurt much by changing the crystal. You can always put the old one back in if the new one doesn't work well.

Back to the subject of voltage, your power supply steps the line voltage (somewhere between 110 and 120 volts) down to 5 volts for all the chips to run on. Actually, the new exotic high-speed chips work on even lower voltages, the theory being that the lower the voltage, the less energy it takes to switch from on to off, and off to on, thus speeding things up.

By the way, what's a turbo TI99/4A?

Digital Dave

I think someone was pulling this following reader's leg, and he fell for it hook, line and sinker. I guess everyone has to start somewhere, and writing a letter to me is a good start, if you have a sense of humor.

Dear Digital Dave,
I've heard a lot about disk crashes. What is this, and how can I use it? Also, what is the difference between OS/2 and DOS? Can they be used on the same Mac machine like an XT, or only on the newer 80386s?

Joe Kalb

Dear Joe,
I think some of your information is a bit scrambled. First of all, disk crashes are very bad, and you can use them by trying real hard not to have one. That is, unless you want to invent a new computer game called Digital Demolition Derby.

The head of your hard drive flies over the disk on a cushion of air as the disk spins at 3600 revolutions per minute. If for some reason the head comes in contact with the disk surface, ka-pow, there goes the whole shooting match.

Don't bounce your computer around, and don't take the lid off the hard drive, and you should be spared this disaster.

Now, what's the difference between OS/2 and DOS? Well, both operating systems were developed and are now being sold by Microsoft, and both systems will run on just about any AT when you buy the generic version of either. DOS will also run on PCs and XTs.

IBM has a special version of both DOS (PC-DOS) and OS/2, though the special version of OS/2 is not available yet. The difference is that PC-DOS will run on most non-IBM clones, while the special version of OS/2 will only work on certain models of the new IBM PS/2 computers, some of which use the 80386 and some the older 80286.

Neither DOS or OS/2 will run on a Macintosh computer, unless the Mac has been equipped with special hardware to emulate a PC. The Mac has its own special operating system by Apple that takes advantage of its graphics capabilities.

Digital Dave

Some people just don't know when to quit. If the trip to the repair shop will cost more than half the purchase price, throw it away! And don't buy another of the same brand. You know, once burned, twice shy?

Dear Digital Dave,
 I've bought two CH Products Mach III joysticks. Each time I bought one, the buttons would not function two weeks after the warranty ran out.
 I took them apart and tried to fix them myself. No luck. It's too expensive to take them somewhere to have them fixed. Do you know where I can buy new buttons for them? I have looked around, but haven't found any.

Bill Scott

Dear Bill,

The easiest thing to do is throw those 'sticks away and buy some new ones, from a different manufacturer, of course. Now what if you are in love with those particular little boxes of joy? Well, the buttons are only switches, after all.

The problem is that the buttons are really *el cheapo*, which no self-respecting switch maker would sell as a separate item. Why not just put in a different switch? You should be able to pick up some real nice military-surplus push-button switches at the local amateur radio swap-fest or electronics surplus store. Even Radio Shack carries some.

Pick a normally open, momentary contact switch, which most push buttons are, that will physically fit in the joystick housing. Get out your drill and soldering iron, or have a hacker friend have at it.

Digital Dave

The next letter comes in all too often. Unfortunately, all computers are subject to failures in the RAM chips, from Apple IIs to Cray supercomputers. It's easy and inexpensive to replace the bad chip. Finding the right one is the problem.

Dear Digital Dave,

I have a Doland 640K XT clone with a 20MB hard disk and a monographic printer card. Eight times lately, while running different programs (DacEasy, Lotus 1-2-3, and PC Tools), I have had my computer lock up on me. A message cuts into the program stating "P-CK 1(M)" and the bell rings until I reboot the computer.

One night this happened three times. Other nights nothing at all happens. Please give me some insight into the problem. I would prefer to not have expensive repair people working on it if it is only a simple problem.

Dale Griffin

Dear Dale,

I'm afraid that it's not a simple problem, and the solution is not cheap, though it is simple. Replace the motherboard. I know you didn't want to hear that. The fact that it happens on more than one program indicates that it's a hardware problem, not just a dropped bit in a disk file. The message you get sounds like the dreaded "MEMORY PARITY ERROR" message that most computers use as their swan song.

This means that the hardware has detected an error in the main memory and doesn't know how to deal with it. A friend of mine has had a similar problem, which I've tried to fix for years. I've swapped the RAM chips and replaced several of the chips that control the memory. It seems to help for a while, then the problem pops up again. Now my computer in my office at work has the problem. About once a week it just locks up, sometimes with the message, and sometimes without.

Either back up your data to disk often, or get a new motherboard and be glad motherboards for XTs don't cost much.

Digital Dave

Running out of memory can look a lot like a bad RAM chip because the program ends up reading a piece of DOS or something else besides its own instructions. It all goes under the same sort of names: crashed, bombed, etc.

Dear Digital Dave,

I have an XT Turbo with a 40MB hard drive and a 360K floppy drive. I have 640K of RAM and run DOS version 3.0.

My problem is this: My PC either locks up or gives a "divide overflow" error message when I run certain programs that require 512K or more of RAM. Will I have to expand my RAM to accommodate the few programs that will not run, or are there other alternatives?

H. F. Smith, Jr.

Dear H. F.,

Now, what can we do about your computer lock-up problem? It's either real easy or real hard.

First the easy one. If you run any programs that stay in memory, such as *Sidekick*, or anything that pops up when you hit a hot key, then try rebooting from a clean DOS disk. Run your over-512K program.

Those Terminate and Stay Resident (TSR) programs take up some of your valuable RAM, even when you're not using them. Between the space DOS itself takes up and those TSRs, you might have used up enough memory out of your 640K so that the larger programs won't fit.

If the 512K program still crashes your computer when it has been booted with only DOS (no TSR), then either you have a hardware problem (real pain to locate and fix) or the copy of the program is damaged.

Oh yes, there is one more possibility. If the program was written under DOS 2.X, and they used up all the possible RAM left over out of 640K, then running it under 3.0 could be a problem. Later versions of DOS tend to take up more RAM space.

Digital Dave

Keeping a watch on your free space can avoid the above problem. Many programs announce how much free space is available. Also many utility programs, such as FREE.COM, do the same.

Dear Digital Dave,

My PC clone has 640K of memory hardware. I have lots of programs on it that run just fine, but when I boot up, one of the programs in the AUTOEXEC.BAT file announces that there is only 354K of free space left. Why is this so?

Spike Harris

Dear Spike,

First off, PC-DOS takes a chunk out of your RAM memory, and you can't do much about that. Another possibility might be that you have a bunch of file buffers set up. Those are the chunks of memory where the programs put and get data on the way to and from the disk.

Now then, what about all those goodies in your AUTO-EXEC.BAT file? Chances are they're what are known as Terminate and Stay Resident or TSR programs. When called, they install themselves in memory and stay there. The next time you need them, they pop right up, usually with a hot key.

Take a look at that long list of programs in your AUTO-EXEC.BAT file. Do you really need them all the time? You can always install them manually when they're needed. That would leave your programs with more breathing room.

Digital Dave

Didn't they make jokes about people wearing out their button-pushing finger when computers took over the world? Well, computers are far from winning the battle, but already there is someone who can't press one button.

Dear Digital Dave,

I recently bought an AT compatible running DOS 3.3, with an AMI BIOS and 1MB of RAM. As a former XT user, I've encountered something that is annoying. Perhaps you have a solution for it.

The new machine defaults to NumLock on. How can I make it default to off? There must be a patch of some sort, as a program I use (Microsoft Show Partner*) turns it off automatically as soon as the program loads.*

Brooks Lyman

Dear Brooks,

This column is going to start sounding like an advertisement for *PC Magazine's DOS Power Tools*. It's a book that
you can pick up at your local bookseller, but it includes a disk
with a bunch (and I mean a bunch) of great utility programs,
along with inside info on your PC.

The disk includes a program called NUM-OFF.COM.
Copy this over to your hard drive and put the NUMOFF
command in your AUTOEXEC.BAT file. Then every time
you boot up, *NumOff* will turn off your NumLock.

Digital Dave

I guess there's room in the world for all types. I can put up with
simpletons and fools, but people who think computer manuals are
easy to understand? Keep them away from me.

Dear Digital Dave,

*I just wanted you to know that I'm one of the rare breed
who finds computer manuals (software and hardware) ex-
ceptionally good. I don't know why so many people com-
plain that these things are poorly written.*

*The information is thorough and complete. In fact, I find
it redundant that there are so many trade books out there,
most of which are rewrites of the manuals. Do you, as a
technical person, think the manuals are well written—or
am I just nuts?*

John Philmer

Dear John,

You're nuts. Now there are a number of very well-docu-
mented software programs on the market, but I can't think of
a piece of hardware with a decent manual.

One extreme is the IBM camp, with their dinky three-ring
binders-in-a-box. Each piece is explained, with a lot of technical jargon, but nothing tells you how the whole thing goes

together. The other end of the street is the Apple Macintosh, with their cutesy-pie smiling and frowning faces and bomb boxes. Even if you figure out how to use it, you never really understand what you're doing.

I do agree that most of the books about computers are not much more than a rehash of the hardware or software manuals. I think the major market is for people who have ripped off the software, but don't have a manual. Anything for a buck. Maybe the people who wrote the software should get a cut of the action to make up for the loss in sales.

I like a manual that is organized as a reference manual. Each command or topic is listed separately and in alphabetical order so I can find them. Each command should have a syntax chart to clearly show all possible forms of the command right up front, then a brief explanation.

All this is great for someone who is already familiar with a software package. But how do you get started? An on-disk interactive tutorial is the only way to go. Tutorials in a book put me to sleep. We're working with a computer, so why not put it to good use?

The one other thing you absolutely need when working with a program like a computer language or a database manager is examples. Lots of little ones, so you can get your feet wet without getting lost, and a few big ones to really get down to the nitty gritty. That's where the tricks of the trade are learned.

Digital Dave

Here is another one of those don't-know-when-to-quit people.

Dear Digital Dave,

Is it possible to pop the key caps off the keyboard of my IBM clone? I need to clean all the potato-chip pieces and hair balls which have accumulated there.

Mary McNally

Dear Mary,

There are so many different types of keyboards for clones, some of which come apart and some of which don't. I would advise you not to take the key caps off unless something is broken.

A friend of mine took his key caps off of his true-blue PC keyboard to rearrange them to the Dvorak layout. He didn't have to pull the space bar off, but he did anyway, just to clean under it. He limped along with a broken keyboard for a few months, until he broke down and bought a new one. There was no way to fix the old one.

I would get a brush, turn the keyboard upside down, and brush out as much of the crud as possible. Then, don't eat potato chips while you're computing. Besides getting chips in between, you get grease all over those pretty white keys, and make the hair balls stick.

Digital Dave

Sometimes it's better to swallow your pride and just let it go. If you got stuck with a bad sale, why try to pawn it off on someone else?

Dear Digital Dave,

I made a terrible mistake when I first bought my computer. The mistake was asking the salesperson what software I needed. He loaded me up with about $600 worth of useless junk.

After paying for that lesson, I've done my homework and now know what I want as far as software goes.

Can I sell that $600 worth of software? A friend tells me it's illegal and I'm stuck with it. If I can't sell it, can I swap it away? I just want to get rid of it (bad memories, you know).

Julie Smith

Dear Julie,

There is no law against selling anything that is yours. The problem is discovering just what you did buy when you forked over 600 bucks. Read the licence agreement that came with the software. In most cases, what you've purchased is the right to use the software.

If the contract was carefully written, there should be some sort of mechanism for transfer of the license. This might require written permission from the software manufacturer.

Now comes the big problem. Who would want to buy a piece of software that's a piece of junk? Could you look your friend in the (bloodshot) eye after he or she spent all night trying to get that junky gift from you to do something useful?

Maybe you'd be better off signing over the license to a charitable organization, like a school, and taking it off your taxes. Check with your tax preparer first.

Digital Dave

INDEX